301

QUESTIONS & ANSWERS

For Every Savvy
Real Estate Investor

Steven VanCauwenbergh
Walter Jenkins

301 Questions & Answers
For Every Real Estate Investor

International Standard Book Number: 978-0-9859805-3-5

Printed in the United States of America

This publication is designed to provide competent and reliable information regarding the subject matter covered for informational purposes. However, it is sold with the understanding that the author and publisher are not engaged in rendering legal, financial, or other professional advice. Laws and practices often vary from state to state and if legal or other expert assistance is required, the services of a professional should be sought. The author and publisher specifically disclaim any liability that is incurred from the use or application of the contents of this book. While every attempt has been made to verify the information in this book, neither the author nor his affiliates/partners assume any responsibility for errors, inaccuracies, or omissions.

Published by Teflon Publishing,
8 NE 48th Street, Oklahoma City, OK 73105
The Savvy Landlord name and logo are trademarks of Teflon Publishing
Library of Congress Cataloging-in-Publication data
is available from the publisher

Interior design by Gorilla Media Group
Cover design by Elizabeth Hunt with Gorilla Media Group
www.gorillamediagroup.com

To Shannez' VanCauwenbergh,

whose support, encouragement, advice

and love has pushed me to the

realization of my dreams.

Contents

"The book you don't read won't help."
- Jim Rohn

INTRODUCTION

I wrote *301 Questions and Answers for Every Savvy Real Estate Investor* because I wanted both newbie and seasoned investors to understand the issues they will face when they build their empires. Knowledge is power, and it gives you the confidence to pull the trigger on your first investment or to do more deals.

I want to empower people to make informed decisions. When you have information you won't feel intimated when you make an offer on a property and won't be too paralyzed to invest.

Almost every question in this book addresses an issue I encountered during my thirteen years as real estate investor. I didn't have a book like this when I started building my portfolio, and I had to learn the answers to most of these questions the hard way. The few remaining questions came from other investors who needed practical information.

Some questions may seem obvious and situational while others are complex. I have tried to break the more challenging ones down to their simplest forms. The answers to one or two of these questions can save you thousands of dollars and untold headaches and will reduce the anxiety you face as you navigate the world of real estate investing.

I welcome feedback and would love to hear your questions or comments about real estate investing and the Savvy Landlord Company. Feel free to contact me at thesavvylandlordbook.com.

Please enjoy this labor of love. And may your next deal be your best deal.

QUESTIONS AND ANSWERS

1. My tenant's spouse/roommate/significant other moved out, and the tenant wants to change the locks. What should I do?

It depends. Is the spouse/roommate/significant other on the lease? If so, you won't be able to take his name off or change the locks unless there is a breach of the lease, or unless he gives you written permission. You never want to take someone off a lease unless you are sure whoever stays on the lease can afford to pay the rent. And be careful about getting involved in other people's domestic situations. Even the best people are at their worst when a relationship is going south, and you don't want to get caught in the crossfire.

2. How do I find deals?

Hustle. The only way to get more deals is to work your butt off. They aren't going to just fall out of the sky and hit you in the head. New deals are the lifeblood of your empire, and if you don't have any in the pipeline your business will never grow. The best ways to find deals are to scour the internet (sites like craigslist can be a goldmine), to search the classified section of your local newspaper, and to write down the telephone numbers listed on "For Sale" signs you see as you drive around town. But nothing beats networking. You will get more deals from the people you know than you will from any other source. Join your local real estate investors association (REIA), talk to other investors, build a good relationship with your bank, and let your friends and family know you are looking for deals. Start looking for an investment realtor who understands the business. You'll be surprised how many deals you will find when you let the people you know send opportunities your way.

3. What does "buy & hold," mean?

A "buy & hold" is purchasing an investment property with the idea of owning it for an extended period of time so that you can earn rental income from it or sell it for a profit after you have made money on it. It's different than a "flip," which is where you buy a property with the idea of selling it quickly. If you have read The Savvy Landlord, you know my experience with flips and that I only buy properties as buy & holds.

4. What's a good average cash flow on a rental property?

As much as possible; I would not do any deal if I did not cash flow at least $100 per month, although $200 is my goal. If I cash flow $300 per month it would be a home run. I have a few properties where I will cash flow substantially more than that after I pay off mortgages, and I hope each and every one of you gets at least one sweet deal like that.

5. Should I partner with someone on a deal?

It depends. Partnering can be a great way to access someone else's money, skill, time, and experience, especially when you are new to the business. But you have to make sure you have the right partner. If you partner with someone, make sure you share the same goals. You don't want to work with someone who doesn't want to grow his business like you want to grow yours. Even the nicest people can be anchors, and you don't want them dragging you down. A partnership can be very stressful, and you both need to understand that going into the deal. You don't want to lose money and a friendship, so if you decide to go into partnerships, choose carefully. And be sure to get everything in writing, including who pays for what, who owns the property, any important deadlines, and how you get paid. If you go into a partnership without a written agreement and things fall apart, you get what you deserve.

6. What does a wholesaler do?

A wholesaler helps real estate investors find deals. They find investment properties and refer them to an investor for a fee. Wholesalers aren't interested in being landlords or they may not have the money to repair or rehab properties. They only want to sell them as quickly as possible and move on to the next deal. You might think of them as micro-flippers.

7. Should I rent to a sex offender?

Sure, and while you are at it, expand the garage so he can build a nice meth lab. I wouldn't recommend renting to sex offenders for many reasons. There might be liability issues if he does something on your property. Plus, most sex offenders have to register with law enforcement agencies, and this information can be found online. You don't want the neighbors who live near your property to find out and for you to get the reputation as someone who brought an offender into their neighborhood. You want to maintain a positive working relationship with the people who own houses near your investments because they can serve as your eyes and ears when you are not around. If you decide to rent to a sex offender, make sure you check with your attorney regarding any responsibilities this may put on you. And be sure to charge a substantial deposit, and visit with your attorney to see if you can make it nonrefundable. You don't want to have a dispute about a refund if a tenant is forced to move because of something he did or failed to do. Only pay for the mistakes you make. Don't take on the burden of underwriting someone else's shortcomings.

8. Does my insurance cover my tenants' personal belongings?

No. Your insurance will only cover your property. If tenants want their belongings insured, they will need to purchase renter's insurance. You might include a recommendation about renter's insurance when tenants sign their leases. The rates are surprising affordable, and a policy can save a lot of headache if anything happens to the property.

9. What's the difference between a Realtor and an investment Realtor?

A Realtor (or retail Realtor) is what most people think of when they hear the word Realtor. It is someone who helps individuals buy homes to live in. An investment Realtor is someone like you, who buys and sells property for investment purposes. When you are looking for a Realtor, either to send you deals or to help you find properties, you would want to find an investment Realtor who understands real estate investing works and what the issues are. Hopefully, he will be as motivated as you are and will help move your business to the fast lane.

10. What's a reasonable amount of earnest money on a contract to purchase?

As little as possible. One of the most important techniques you will use to grow your empire is to leverage your money. You want to take a small amount of money and use it to borrow more money. You should spend as little of your own money as possible and spend as much of other people's money (OPM) as possible. However, when you do have to put down earnest money, it shouldn't be more than 5 to 10 percent of the purchase price. I usually put down $1,000, which looks a lot more attractive than the normal $500 most investors put down.

11. When should I build a relationship with a bank?

Hopefully, you started building a relationship with your bank before you did your first deal. Being able to look your banker in the eye and tell him about your goals and why you need to borrow money is very important. My banker has even referred me deals because of the relationship we have formed. My business wouldn't be where it is today if I hadn't taken the time to get to know my banker and to keep him in the loop with my deals. But it's never too late to start a relationship with the people who loan you money. Take a few moments to call your banker and ask if you can drop by his office and get to know him a little bit. Once you know each other, take him out to lunch and get to know each other as people. It's one of the best investments you will ever make.

12. Should I dye the carpet in my rental property?

You probably shouldn't be using carpet at all. Laminate floors are cheaper to install, easier and less expensive to maintain, and last longer than carpets. You're throwing money away if you keep using carpets instead of laminate. If your tenants want carpeting, they can buy floor rugs. But if you do use carpets you can dye them to hide stains you can't remove or to extend the life of the carpet.

13. How do I calculate my ROI on a deal?

You should start calculating ROI before you buy any property. It's one of the best ways to make sure your investments are profitable. To calculate ROI, in a property, take your monthly cash flow, multiply it by twelve (it is based on annual amounts) and divide that by the equity you have in the property. For example, if you cash flow $300 after taxes and expenses on a house you have $25,000 invested in you would divide $3,600 by $25,000, which equals 14.4 percent.

14. What's a good amount I should set aside for repairs, vacancies, and make-readies?

A good rule of thumb is to have six months set aside for insurance, taxes, and mortgage payments on each property. Real estate investing is a great way to build wealth, but it can be uncertain at times. Be savvy and keep enough money in the bank to stay afloat during tough times.

15. Can I really buy a house with no money down?

Yes, and you can even do it where you leave the closing with a check from the equity your acquired in the property. The key is to find properties that are available at prices below their appraised values. My bank loans at 70 percent of the appraised value, so if I find a property with a really motivated seller, I can get a loan for more than the asking price, and that means I don't have any of my cash in the deal. I once bought a house that was appraised at $95,000 for $50,000, and then took out a mortgage on it for $60,000. That left me with $10,000 to play with. There's nothing better than leaving a closing with cash from the equity in your new property.

16. Are those real estate gurus really worth the money they charge for their programs?

Yes and no. Some of those gurus are seasoned investors who present a lot of valuable material in an entertaining and educational manner. But some of them don't know what they are talking about and it's painful to sit through their programs. If you are serious about building wealth with real estate, or want to transform your real estate business into a real estate empire, you have to educate yourself. You have to learn as much as you can, and that includes reading, joining your local REIA, finding a mentor and asking as many questions as possible, and it may include going to seminars. I know successful investors who have attended or purchased seminars from several gurus, and I know others who have never used them. There is no cookie cutter approach to this. You have to find what works for you. The only wrong answer is to do nothing and to refuse to accept responsibility for your education. Eventually, you have to get off the couch and get to work. The best education is on the job training.

17. Should I tell people I am a landlord, a real estate investor, and/or the next Donald Trump apprentice?

It's okay for you to talk to your friends, family, and your banker about what you do. It's a great profession, and you should be proud you are a part of it. But if you call yourself the owner or landlord in front of your tenants, you are asking for trouble. To some people, that means you have a lot of money and once they think that they start looking at you as their next meal ticket. Unfortunately, we live in a culture where some people are quick to sue, especially when they think people with money will pay to make lawsuits go away, regardless of how frivolous their claim is. Spare yourself the headache by not calling yourself the landlord or investor. Pick a better word, such as "manager."

18. Should I work on the houses myself or hire someone?

Start hiring people to do the work for you as soon as possible. A common mistake new investors make is to think they have to do all the painting, cleaning, and labor intensive tasks themselves. It's easy to tell yourself that you can't justify the cost of hiring people to do these things, and that's true for many investors when they buy their first few properties. Plus, doing some of that work yourself is a great way to learn what needs to be done and how much time is involved. But as your empire grows, you need to learn to farm that work out. If you try to save a few bucks by painting all your houses yourself, it's going to cost you money in the long run. I know one investor who cost himself $30,000 by trying to save a few hundred bucks when didn't want to hire someone to paint a house. Don't let that happen to you. Hire people to do work for you so you can focus on bringing in new deals. Your time is much more valuable than the $10 or $20 an hour it will cost to get this work done.

19. Should I rent my property to a family member?

Only if you want to be miserable at family reunions, weddings, and Christmas parties. If everything goes well, renting to family members can be a great experience. You know who they are and can be confident they will pay their rent on time. After all, you've known Aunt Susie and Cousin Billy your entire life and they have always been good to you. But what happens when Susie loses her job and can't pay her rent? What if there is an issue with the plumbing and you are not able to get it fixed quickly enough to keep Cousin Billy happy? Not only will you have to deal with an unhappy tenant, you may also get stared down by your grandmother, your brother, and/or all of your nieces and nephews. It's not worth the headache to do business with family. Avoid it at all costs.

20. Should I only buy investment properties with cash?

No, and if you are buying all of your properties with cash you are making a mistake. The key to building wealth in real estate is leveraging your money, and that means using as much OPM (other people's money) as you can. Plus, if you pay with cash you won't be able to take many of the deductions you are entitled to, including interest on mortgage payments. Use your cash to make down payments on several different properties instead of tying it up in one property. That's the way savvy landlords build real wealth.

21. Should I buy a home warranty on a house I bought as an investment?

I never buy home warranties because I can't justify the cost on my properties. It doesn't make economic sense. But it may work for you. Be sure to factor in the cost when you crunch the numbers before you buy the property. Your cash flow will be determined the day you buy your property and if you don't get the numbers right then you may never make money.

22. What does "as is" really mean?

"As is" is code for, "This house is a real dog. It needs a lot of work. If you spend too much for it, you may never recoup the purchase price and the expense of rehabbing it. Only a sucker or a newbie would buy this property without understanding how much money you will have to throw at it before you can rent it." You can make a great living buying houses listed "as is," but you need to understand the costs involved. Those two words are a red flag, and you need to make sure you do your due diligence before you write a check for an "as is" house.

23. What do I do when the house I bought turned out to be a bad deal?

So you bought a property and it wasn't the gem you thought it would be? Welcome to the club. It happens to all of us and it's not the end of the world. The most important thing to do when you realize you made a bad deal is to understand where things went wrong. Did you pay too much for the property? Were there issues with one of the systems (plumbing, electrical, or foundation) that didn't show up when you did your due diligence? Did you rush into the deal? Once you have an idea of what happened, you need to come up with a game plan. Call your mentor or an investor or two you trust to get an idea of what you need to do. Should you cut your losses, sell the property and move on? Maybe you should invest in repairs to get the house rent ready. Or maybe you need to leave things as they are and ride it out. I've done all three, and there is no right or wrong answer. You have to make a decision as to how you are going to proceed, and then stick with it. The worst thing you can do is to feel sorry for yourself and not take any action at all.

24. What's a good timeframe for rehabbing a house?

As quickly as possible. You can't rent a property until a rehab is done, and if you can't rent it out you won't generate any cash flow from it even though you're paying for the mortgage, insurance, and taxes. Several factors can impact how long it takes to do a rehab. How much work needs to be done? Are you putting on a new roof, rewiring the property, and redoing the plumbing? Or do you just need to do one of these? The amount of work that needs to be done will impact how long it takes. But in general a rehab shouldn't take more than four to six weeks. If it does, make sure your contractor or handymen can explain what's taking so long. And be sure to get the completion date in writing and make sure there are consequences if the work is not done on time, such as a reduction in his fee.

25. What are holding costs?

Holding costs are the costs of owning property for a specified period of time. These generally include the mortgage, taxes, insurance, and maintenance. It's important to understand these issues because once you buy a property; you will always be responsible for the holding costs. If no one is renting the property, you have expenses but no cash flow. Always factor holding costs into the price of buying a new property.

26. I want to be a good landlord. Should I cut the grass for my tenants?

Only if you also agree to wash their dishes, do their laundry, and make hot chocolate for them when it gets cold (be sure to ask if they want those little marshmallows or not). We never cut the grass for our residents. It's in our leases that lawn care is the tenant's responsibility. They need to cut it themselves or they can hire someone to do it for them.

27. A prospective tenant can't get the utilities in his name. Should I put them in my name and let the tenant pay for them when the rent is due each month?

No. Never hand the keys over to a new tenant unless he can prove the utilities are turned on and in his name before he takes possession. You don't want to be responsible for a monster utility bill if the tenant pulls a midnight move and leaves you high and dry. If a tenant can't get the utilities in his name, you should see a giant red flag warning you about all the trouble you will have trouble with him in the future. Avoid the headache by not renting to him.

28. Do you take Section 8?

Yes. Section 8 can be a great way to build your empire. Section 8 is a government program that helps people pay their rent. It is based on several factors, including the renter's income and the number of children living in the home. It can help you guarantee a steady income. Make sure to verify the amount the tenant pays before you sign the lease. You want his portion to be as small as possible and the government's portion to be as large as possible. You will also have to get your properties inspected before you can accept Section 8 tenants.

29. What if the tenant goes to jail?

Tell him to hire a good lawyer. Then make sure your investment is secure. If the police had to kick in the door or knock out any windows, get your handyman over as soon as possible to repair the damage. If there is more than one person on the lease, confirm that the other renters know what has happened. Leave it up to them to notify the tenant's family and job. If the tenant lived by himself, make sure the property is locked and that the stove is off. You might (although you don't have to) call the numbers he listed on his application and let them know what happened. But even that can be tricky. You don't want to get blamed if the tenant gets fired for being arrested. Make sure to drive by and inspect the property if no one is going to be living there. A tenant may call you and beg for you to post his bail. Never, ever, do this. You are only asking for trouble. If he is still in jail when the rent is due, document everything and start the eviction process.

30. What if a tenant dies in one of my properties?

Hopefully, you will not have to endure a tragedy like this. But if a tenant dies in one of your properties, the first thing you should do is call 911. Let the authorities handle it from there. They can investigate if they need to and notify the tenant's next of kin. If they need contact information from your lease, be sure to cooperate. Don't do anything with the tenant's personal property until you have a court order. You don't want to get caught in the middle of a nasty dispute in probate court if his heirs allege you stole the priceless work of art that used to hang on their dad's bedroom wall. Take pictures of the personal property in the house, and document everything you do.

This next thought is morbid, but it is something you need to be prepared for. When people die (even if it is peacefully in their sleep), things fall apart quickly. It won't be long before the body starts smelling and fluids start oozing out. And if the death went undiscovered for a few days, bugs will start taking over. It's a disgusting image, I know, but it's something you need to consider. And if the person committed suicide, was murdered, or had an accident (such as a slip and fall), there might be blood or other things that need to be cleaned up. In the last few years, some entrepreneurs have made a lot of money with companies that specialize in cleaning up crime scenes and places where people have died. You might do a quick Internet search to find one in your area. I hope you never need it, but it's better to have the information in advance.

31. Should I let the tenant paint the property a color of his choosing?

We never let our tenants paint a property, especially the exteriors. You don't want to have an upset neighbor call you because your tenant has painted your house lime green with orange polka dots. To make it easy on us, we paint all of our houses the same color. That way, we only have to find one can of paint if we need to do some touchup work. If you do let a tenant paint the interior, make sure his deposit is large enough to cover the costs of having it repainted. You don't want to be stuck with the tab if he moves out in the middle of the night.

32. What do I do if the tenant allows additional people to live on the property?

Tell the tenant she has breached her lease in writing and start documenting your conversation. You need to know who is living in your properties. If the tenant lets the wrong people into your investment, you could face liability issues or be stuck with the costs of repairing damage caused by a bunch of knuckleheads you never would have let near the house. We also have a clause in our lease that requires the tenant to pay an additional $100 per month if she allows other people to live on the property. Letting additional people live in the house is a giant red flag. If the tenant is willing to breach her agreement on this issue, she will breach it on others. Hopefully, once you send her a letter she will get rid of the baggage. If not, you'll be ready to start evicting her.

33. What if my tenant brings a pet home without telling me?

If he is that excited about having a pet, tell him to volunteer at a rescue shelter. We don't allow pets, and it's spelled out in our lease. If you decide to allow pets, you shouldn't let your tenants have any that weigh more than forty pounds. Large animals cause a lot of wear and tear on property, and they are not worth the trouble from a landlord's perspective. If you allow pets, make sure to charge a deposit large enough to pay for a cleanup. We charge a $250 non-refundable deposit.

34. What happens when I purchase a property with a tenant in it already?

Holdover tenants are a blessing and a curse. They can give you cash flow from the first day you own a property, but they can cause you headaches and give you nightmares if the previous owner has rented to the wrong people or if he has not done his job. Before you buy a property, review the payment history of any tenants you will inherit. You want to know if any of them are going to be speed bumps on your way to the fast lane. Make sure the seller has complete and accurate contact information and iden-tification information, such as Social Security Numbers and birthdates. If you have to take legal action, you'll be screwed if you don't have basic information like that. Review the leases to see if there are any surprises, and make sure the tenants are paying market value. Once you buy the prop-erty, introduce yourself to your new tenants and have a face-to-face meeting with them. To be professional, send a letter introducing yourself and giving them your contact information so they know how to get in touch with you and where to send the rent. Explain your expectations and what will hap-pen if the rent is not paid on time. When the meeting is over, the tenants should understand that you are professional and that you are going to run the property like a business. Just because the previous owner was lax about things doesn't mean you will be.

35. My Realtor refuses to submit an offer on a property. What should I do?

What's the problem? Is she allergic to money? Is she afraid of moving into a higher tax bracket? The first thing you need to do is to ask her what the problem is. Maybe it is just miscommunication. Or maybe she thinks she can get you a better deal on the property and is stalling as a negotiating tactic. If it turns out she is refusing to submit the offer and just won't do it, you need to document her refusal and end your relationship with her as quickly as possible. She's not going to help build your empire unless she is willing to submit as many offers as possible, and if she won't do that you need to find someone who will. That may sound harsh, but she is either helping you get on the fast lane or she is an obstacle between you and your goals. And if that's the case, you need to send her on her way.

36. How much repair is too much?

This is a trap a lot of new investors fall into. They buy a property to rent and think they have to fix every tiny detail and give the property every bell and whistle possible. Investors have two goals when they repair properties. The first is to protect their investments. You have to repair the major systems, like the roof, plumbing, and the wiring. If you don't take care of those, your property will start crumbling beneath you and you will lose every penny you put in it. The second goal you have with repairs is to provide a place for your tenants to live that is habitable and that justifies the rent you are charging. Don't think that you have to repair your properties as if you were going to live there. And be sure to keep any necessary repairs within your budget. Keep it simple, do the basics, and watch your empire grow.

37. How do I find a good contractor?

You will need to build a team of qualified people to help you maintain your properties, and finding a good contractor is an important part of this. One of the best ways to find a good contractor is to talk to other investors you know and trust. But don't be surprised if they slow roll you and won't give up names easily. Good help is hard to find and a lot of us don't want to lose our contractors. Another good place to start is Craigslist. Run a Craigslist add for contractors and you will be surprised at how many people will respond. Interview the ones you feel the most comfortable with, and be sure to check their references. Always trust but verify.

38. What does "flipper" mean?

We're not talking about super-smart dolphins with their own TV shows. A flipper is an investor who buys a property and sells it quickly for a profit. Flippers are not interested in being landlords. They just want to make a quick profit and then move on to the next deal. Flippers are different from holders, who buy property and hold on to it for a long time so they can rent it and eventually sell it.

39. Should I have the tenant purchase renter's insurance?

You can't force tenants to buy renter's insurance. But you can educate them about their options. When we meet with our tenants before they sign their leases, we let them know that renter's insurance is available and that they should consider purchasing it. It's not very expensive (some polices are as low as $12 per month), and a policy will make it easier for everybody if your property is damaged. You want your tenants to get back on their feet as quickly as they can after a fire, earthquake, or tornado because it's the right thing to do. But it also helps your cash flow. Your empire won't grow if your tenants are looking for a new place to live because they lost everything they own in a fire and are trying to make you pay for it.

40. Can tenants park on the grass?

No. Most cities have outlawed people parking on the grass. It looks tacky and will probably piss off your neighbors. Unless you want to be the butt of "You might be a redneck if . . . ." jokes, put a clause in the lease specifically stating that tenants cannot park on the grass.

41. Should I allow a tenant to store his RV on the property for two weeks?

I wouldn't be excited about this. You don't want to do anything that makes the property look cheap or interferes with your neighbors' ability to use and enjoy their homes. Where would he park the RV? Is it too big to fit in the driveway? If it is parked on the street, will it block any driveways and will cars be able to maneuver around it? It would probably be best for the tenant to find somewhere else to park his land yacht. Plus, most cities have made it illegal to park RVs on the streets, which is good for you because you don't have to be the bad guy.

42. The tenant wants a fence for the backyard. Should I buy it?

Fencing in backyards can be a great investment. People (especially families with kids) will pay more for properties with fenced-in backyards. But you have to do it when it makes sense to you and not just because a tenant wants it done. If you pay for the fence, how will it impact your cash flow? Will it make the deal to skinny? Remember that once you install the fence, you have to maintain it, and you need to factor that into your costs. Is the tenant willing to pay additional rent to cover the cost of installing the fence? Don't put the fence up unless it fits into your overall investing strategy.

43. My tenant is requesting an automatic garage door opener. Should I pay for it?

Again, this can be a great investment that will attract better tenants to your properties. But don't pay for it (and the maintenance that comes with it) unless you crunch the numbers and they make sense. And be sure that the value of items like this are reflected in the rent.

44. My tenant requests safety grab bars to be installed in the bathroom. Should I allow this?

Yes, in fact, depending on the circumstances, you may be required to. If the tenant has a medical condition that qualifies as a disability, there may be federal, state, or local rules and regulations that force you to install the bars. Paying for a few bars to be installed is a small price to pay to do the right thing and make sure you follow the law. It's not always the best thing to do your investment, but it's the right thing and tenants are willing to pay for it.

45. Can I give an extra key to one of my rental properties to my girlfriend?

Not today, not tomorrow, not ever. The only people who should ever have keys to any of your rental properties are you, your tenants, and your management team or the contractors you hire to work on the properties. No one should ever have a key to one of your properties without a valid business reason. You should be able to account for every key at all times or you are asking for trouble. Girlfriends have a way of becoming ex-girlfriends, and you don't want to be in the awkward situation of tracking down your ex (or paying for new locks) because she thinks you did her wrong and refuses to return the key. Plus, controlling the keys allows you to protect your friends and girlfriends. If they never had a key they can never be falsely accused of entering the property and taking something. Don't put your friendship or business at risk. Don't give away keys to anyone without a business reason.

46. My tenant wants to be his own landlord and asked if it's okay to rent out his spare bedroom. What should I do?

If he wants to be a landlord, he can get off his butt, find some properties, and start an investment company just like you did. He doesn't need to cut his teeth at your expense. Your lease should clearly state that subletting is prohibited, and when he calls to ask you about it you should read it to him word for word. Then document your conversation with a letter and follow up to make sure no one else is living on the property. There may be a situation where the tenant gets married or wants someone else living with him, and if you approve and they sign a new lease that's fine. But the only people who live on your properties should be the ones you approve of and who are on the lease. If someone else moves in, it should be with your approval and not because the tenant did it on his own.

47. What appliances come with the property?

I keep it simple and only include a stove. If you are savvy, you can find a way to make money with appliances. I rent out refrigerators for $25 a month. As you buy more and more properties, you will start to accumulate extra stoves and refrigerators. You can buy used ones for about $150. You can rent them to tenants and apply the money toward your next investment property. It may not sound like much, but if you multiply those dollars over dozens (or hundreds) of properties, it can add up to some serious cash. Always keep your eyes open for money-making opportunities like this.

48. A tenant just called in tears and said he lost his job. What should I say?

This is a delicate area. You want to be comforting and sympathetic, but you have to remember that owning property is a business. Don't allow yourself to get sucked into someone else's personal problems. Ask the tenant if he has any friends or family he could call. If you know of any organizations that help people with financial assistance when they are going through tough times, refer the tenant to them. You want to do the right thing by helping the tenant, and it's cheaper to keep an existing tenant than it is to find a new one. Do what you can to help out without being a doormat.

49. My tenant is the military and he just got called up. What do I do?

Start by thanking him for his service. This can be a pretty tricky area, and you should consult with your attorney when you start investing to make sure you understand what your responsibilities are when you rent to the awesome men and women who serve in the military. Federal laws known as "Service Members Civil Relief Act" protect military family members. The short version is that service members who are called up to active duty are allowed to terminate residential leases. They have to do it in writing and it doesn't take effect for a few weeks, but the bottom line is they can probably get out of the lease and there is nothing you can do, except get the property ready for the next tenant. It's a small price to pay to honor the men and women who serve us. Some places have enacted laws that require you to search a database and ensure that your tenant is not in the military before you evict him. Make sure you visit with your attorney about this so that you know what you need to do when you rent to soldiers.

50. My tenant's lease is ending next month what do I do?

The first thing you need to do is to figure out what the tenant is going to do. Has he given you a thirty-day notice? Is it clear if he is staying or going? If he wants to stay, you need to get him to sign a new lease (Assuming, of course, you want to keep him as a tenant). If he wants to leave, you should mail him a letter explaining when you will return his deposit. Two weeks before the tenant moves out inspect the property and mail a letter detailing any repairs that will have to be made including the cost of the repairs. The week before he moves out, call and remind him of his move-out date and encourage him to have the property in tip-top shape. If he doesn't, he won't get his full deposit back. I included some great forms in the back of The Savvy Landlord, and you can find a "Lease Addendum" for your review. This will make it easier for you and your tenant to renew a lease.

51. My tenant wants to be green and raise his own chickens. Should I let him raise livestock on the property?

There is a special place for people who want to raise chickens and milk cows. It's called the country. Your tenant should look into it. I don't know why, but for some reason, the idea of "urban farming" has been gaining momentum over the course of the last few years. People want to raise livestock and grow vegetables even when they live in the heart of the city. I don't know about you, but I don't want to live next to a flock of chickens and the mess they create, and most of your neighbors won't either. If your tenants want to be farmers, they can live somewhere else.

52. A prospective tenant with a felony conviction for murder wants to rent from me. What should I do?

I believe in second chances. I have made my fair share of mistakes, and I am glad that people looked past my shortcomings and gave me chances. And I believe that others people deserve second chances, too. But when someone with a violent felony conviction tries to rent one of your properties, you need to be extremely cautious. You need to know more of the facts. Has the tenant been out of jail for several years and demonstrated a history of employment and staying out of trouble? Or did he see one of your "For Rent" signs today when he was hitchhiking to his mom's house after being released from prison? Unless someone can show me he has changed, I would have a hard time renting property to him. There is too much liability and too much to lose. Your time is too valuable. Be careful who you rent to and you will avoid most of the problems that landlords deal with.

53. My tenant just called and they are locked out. What should I do?

Your lease should state that you charge for lockout calls. If you don't, you will get more of these calls than you can handle, and you won't get a good night's sleep. Make sure this "stupid tax" is high enough (I would say at least $25 per call) to make sure the tenant learns a lesson. If you don't charge for it or if the fee is too low, the tenant won't feel any pain and you'll never get him to remember his keys. We've taken it one step further. We are replacing the self-locking door knobs with deadbolts. The only way the door can be locked is with a key. This is going to save us time and trouble, and we won't have to get out of bed to unlock doors.

54. A perspective tenant put a deposit and then two weeks later changed her mind. What do I do?

Every time someone gives you a deposit, make them sign a piece of paper that states you are receiving the deposit in exchange for guaranteeing the property will be available by a certain date. If you fail to make the property available on time, the tenant is entitled to a refund. If the tenant changes her mind, she doesn't get the money back. There is no refund if she changes her mind or fails to move in for any reason. We have a free form available at thesavvylandlordbook.com.

55. My tenant pays his rent in cash every month. Do I have to deposit the money in the bank?

A savvy landlord will create a paper trail a mile wide and three feet deep and won't accept cash payments. If you accept cash and don't deposit the money, you will still have to account for it when tax season rolls around. Plus, you want to include it in your financial statements when you apply for a loan or sell your business. You want your business to look as healthy as possible, and you can't do that if you don't deposit every rent payment into your company account. Dealing in cash looks squirrely to a lot of people, and it can cause practical problems. What if a tenant doesn't pay you, but when you try to evict him, he tells the judge he paid you in cash? A few dollars "under the table" can cost you a multimillion-dollar empire. Be as transparent as possible and document everything. You'll sleep better at night.

56. I am processing a tenant's lease, but when I asked for his Social Security Number he didn't want to give it to me. What should I do?

Tear up the application and look for another tenant if he won't give you his SSN. If you are serious about making money, you have to prepare for the times that things don't go as you planned. And that means being able to track down people who owe you money. Most of the people who rent from you will pay their rent on time and will live up to the terms of their leases. But a few people will take advantage of you, and this includes not paying rent. Eventually, someone will move out when they owe you money, and if you don't have as much information as possible, you may never be able to find him or get paid. Don't process an application without the prospect's full name, date of birth, SSN, and driver's license number. And make photocopies of a picture ID. You will thank me later.

57. I have been reading about the Fair Housing Act and I'm really intimidated. Do I have to rent to everyone who likes my property?

No, but this can be complicated and you should visit with your attorney to make sure you understand the Fair Housing Act. It's a lot cheaper to pay for an office visit than it is to hire her to defend you against a frivolous lawsuit. Basically, what the Act says is that you can't refuse to rent to people because of their race, religion, disability, and several other protected classes. If you won't rent to people for one of those reasons, you can be on the receiving end of a juicy lawsuit. The only color that should matter to you as a landlord is green. You're in the game to make money, and it doesn't matter who rents your properties as long as he pays on time and lives up to the terms of the lease. If you have issues dealing with people who are different than you, do us all a favor and look for another line of work. You'll only get yourself in trouble and make the rest of us look bad.

58. A prospective tenant only has $200 of the $900 deposit. Should I let him pay out the deposit?

Nope. This is a major red flag, and if you rent to this person, you deserve what you get. He hasn't even signed the lease yet and he's already behind. How is it going to get any better two months from now? Don't start your relationship by creating a situation where nobody can win. If a prospect can't pay the deposit, he probably won't be able to pay the rent. Wait for someone better to come along.

59. One of my long-term tenants just had her leg amputated and expects me to build a ramp for her wheel chair. What should I do?

You may not be legally required to make the changes for her, but you would have to allow her to make the changes. But you want to do the right thing. If she has been a long-term tenant, she's paid her rent on time and hasn't breached her lease, I would do as many reasonable things as I could to keep her in the property. How much is it worth to keep a good tenant in one of your houses? How much will it cost to find a new tenant if she moves to a place with a ramp? It's your call, but building a ramp for her may be a great investment.

60. My tenant claims to be a handyman. Should I let him do chores in exchange for rent?

This sounds like a great idea, but it almost never works out. There are several problems with this. You can't buy food or clothes with chores. What happens if his work is shoddy? What if you have to evict him and he tells the judge he paid the rent by mowing the yard or fixing the fence? Tenants should pay the rent by writing a check each month, and you should pay for work that needs to be done with cash or a check. Trying to do it any other way will eventually cause problems; life is too short to go around making trouble for yourself.

61. My tenant just broke up with her boyfriend, and she told me she is moving out. She wants her deposit back. What should I do?

If you've done your homework, you had her sign paperwork stating the deposit guaranteed the property would be available on a certain date. As long as you lived up to your end of that agreement, the deposit is yours to keep. Even if you don't have a signed agreement, I believe you should never refund a deposit when you lived up to your end of the bargain. Why should you pay for someone else's mistake or the fact that her circumstances changed and she is choosing to no longer honor her commitment? Don't let that money leave your account.

62. After living in my property for two weeks, my tenant informed me he is a registered sex offender and can't live within 100 yards of a school. He has to move. Should I give him his deposit back?

If you read The Savvy Landlord, you know this really happened to me. At the time, I was a total newbie and was stunned to learn that the tenant was a sex offender. Up until that time, I thought he was a great guy. I wasn't thinking clearly and agreed to give him his money back. If that were to happen today, there would be no way he would get a refund. I can't emphasize this enough: don't refund money when you haven't done anything wrong. And be sure to draft an agreement that every new tenant signs stating the deposit is to make sure the property is available at a certain time. If the property is good to go at that time, the money is yours to keep regardless of what choices the tenant makes.

63. Do I have to have attorney represent me when filing an eviction?

No, you can learn to do them yourself. I handle every eviction for our company. But evictions can be technical, and you have to make sure you file the right paperwork at the right time and follow the deadlines for your state. If you mess up on one deadline, it can delay your ability to force a tenant out, and this jacks up your cash flow. If you want to handle evictions yourself, you might consider hiring an attorney to do one or two so you can learn the process. Or pay for an office visit and your attorney can teach you how to do them. Once you understand the process, you won't feel overwhelmed and will strut through the courthouse like you own it.

64. We just had a major hailstorm. Should I call the insurance adjuster and file claims for my roofs?

Yes. Part of your job is to preserve and protect your assets. A damaged roof can allow water to leak in, and water is one of your biggest enemies. A small leak can quickly turn into rotten decking, ruined insulation, and moldy drywall. And if those things happen your tenants may be able to break the lease and the value of your asset will drop like crazy. Call the adjuster as soon as you can, get any needed repairs done, and keep your investments safe. That's why you pay for insurance. Don't be afraid to use it when you need it.

65. My tenant's refrigerator stopped working and he expects me to pay for the spoiled food. Should I fork over the cash?

We avoid this issue by not providing refrigerators anymore. Our tenants have to buy or rent them. If you do rent refrigerators, have your tenants sign a release stating you are not liable for any food that rots if the compressor goes out. Renting appliances to tenants can be a great way to make money, but you have to make sure the headaches don't outweigh the money you make each month.

66. My tenant just bought a 60-inch LCD TV and asked if it's okay to mount a satellite dish on the roof. Should I let him?

I see a lot of satellite dishes mounted to houses. I don't know if the owners or tenants did those, but I would not let a resident install one on any of my investments properties. Instead, they can pay for a pole to be put in the backyard and the dish can be mounted to that. There's no need to damage a roof so your tenant can get 748 channels of high-definition TV.

67. My tenant's dog just jumped through the screen door. Should I charge the tenant for repairing it?

Yes. Part of owning a pet is being responsible for it when it breaks things. The tenant needs to pay for the damage. Of course, he can always bill the dog for it, if that makes him feel better. But that's between him and his pet. Keep your nose out of it.

68. The plumber just called me and said that the sewer line at one of my properties was clogged because feminine hygiene products blocked the line. Should I charge the tenant for the service call?

Yes. You are responsible for providing working toilets and drains. Over time, drain pipes my get blocked by tree roots or even crack, and you would be responsible for making those repairs. But you generally not are responsible if the pipe is clogged because foreign objects (such as hygiene products, toys, and paper towels) have been flushed down the drain.

69. The plumber called and found a toy in the washing machine drain line. Should I charge the tenant for the service call?

Yes. A toy is clearly a foreign object, and it would be the tenant's responsibility to pay for it. If the toys are really that dirty, they should be hand-washed, anyway.

70. The tenant claims there is mold in the house and requests a mold test to be done. What should I do?

Ask a few questions and inspect the property. Don't take the tenant's word for it. Your lease should include a clause regarding mold, which states that you have never lived in the house and you have no knowledge about mold. When you did your move-in inspection, it should have been thorough enough that you would have seen any mold in obvious places, such as the bathroom. If there is mold and it's the result of the tenant's actions, such as failing to clean the bathroom, he is responsible for it. But a key issue will be your knowledge of the mold. When did you become aware of it? If you knew of the mold before a tenant moved into your property, you will probably have to pay to have it removed. When you do find out about mold, make sure it is taken care of as quickly as possible. Mold, like water, can wreak havoc on your investment, and you want to get the problem resolved immediately. You can find a mold release form on our website, thesavvy-landlord.com.

71. My tenant is on Section 8. The government pays $423 of the $500 rent, but the tenant can't pay his $77 this month. What should I do?

Issues like this are a pain in the butt. It's not enough money to go to court over, but you can't let the issue slide. You have to nip the problem in the bud before it gets any worse. I would start by documenting the issue. If you have to evict the tenant, you want to make sure you cover all your bases. I would also talk to the tenant, and follow that up with a letter. Why is he having trouble paying his share this month? Is it a temporary situation that will be resolved before the rent is due next month? Or has something changed in the tenant's life that will make it difficult for him to pay the rent going forward? How long has he been a tenant? I might be willing to work with a long-term tenant with a stable payment history more than I would with someone who has only lived in the property for a few weeks. Section 8 can be a sweet deal and you don't want to do anything rash that could cause a hiccup in your cash flow.

72. My tenant signed a twelve-month lease but she wants to the break the lease. She only has one month left. What should I do?

Collect the final month's rent, and smile while you do it. When people sign an agreement it should mean something. You lived up to your end of the deal and you deserve to be paid. Her circumstances may have changed, but that doesn't mean it's okay for her take money out of your pocket. Honor your agreements and expect others to do the same.

73. My tenant's boyfriend kicked in her back door. What should I do?

Once the police leave, make sure the property is secure. If your handyman can't get to the property to fix the door, hire someone else to install another door or to at least put a piece of plywood up until you can hang a new door. It sounds harsh, but don't let yourself get sucked into someone else's personal problems. Focus on your priority, which is to protect your asset. And, yes, you need to charge your tenant for the repairs.

74. My tenant's house was just broken into. What should I do?

Make sure the police have been notified and then secure the property. Don't enter the house if you have any doubts that the burglars could still be inside. After an event like this, it can be easy to let your emotions come into play, but stay focused on your empire. Don't make the situation worse by getting caught up in the moment. Make sure that you document any damage to the property and notify your insurance company.

75. What do I do when a tenant offers to pay for the rent with personal favors?

Turn it down. Cash is king in this business, and nothing else matters. If it's not green and you can't fold it and put it in your pocket, it doesn't matter. Can you pay your phone bill or buy food with a tenant's personal favor? Nope. It's fine to have friends and to do favors for them, but it doesn't work in the real estate business. Stick to deals where you get paid with currency.

76. A married couple just inquired about one of our properties. They both work at cash-based businesses. The husband is a DJ at the strip club where his wife is one of the dancers. What should I do?

It doesn't matter to me how people make money, as long as it's legal. I would be more concerned about their payment history. How long have they lived at their current residence? Have they paid their rent on time? How long have they held their jobs? I remember how bankers looked at me when I made my living as a DJ, and I won't treat other people that way. But I still want to verify that my tenants can and will pay their rent on time. As long as they can document that, I would welcome them with open arms.

77. My tenant said she gave me a thirty-day notice when she dropped of her rent last month. We never saw it. What do I do because I don't have it in writing?

In most places, if the lease has expired the parties are automatically on a month-to-month agreement. Document the fact that you didn't receive the letter so you can start the clock ticking if you want to get rid of her. If she has been a good tenant and you want to keep her, use the time to convince her to stay as a tenant. If it's time for her to go, give her a thirty-day notice and get ready for the next tenant.

78. It's December and I really want to impress my tenants. What kind of Christmas gift should I give them?

If you really want to impress them, buy them solid gold Bentleys with diamond-encrusted headlights. That will be a Christmas they will never forget. Don't worry about impressing your tenants with holiday gifts. Impress them by providing them clean, safe places to live and by taking care of any problems as quickly as you can. If you want to give them something nice during the holidays, a Christmas card with a sincere greeting is always a great gesture.

79. How do I convince my tenants I am not a millionaire?

Unfortunately, when you become successful, some people start scheming. They spend all of their time plotting ways to get your money. You can avoid this by not telling people you own the property. Refer to yourself as the manager or the property manager. If you brag about how many units you own or how much money you make, you probably get what you deserve.

80. Should I install a security system in a property where my tenant continues to leave his children unsupervised?

No. Your obligation is to provide habitable housing for a competitive price. You don't have to do anything beyond that. You can't get caught up in a tenant's personal problems, even when children are involved. Stick to the basics and focus on building your empire.

81. I was cleaning up after a tenant broke his lease and I found several hundred dollars of cash in a drawer. Should I give it back?

Yes. In fact, it may be a crime if you don't. Even if someone owes you money, you do not have the right to take his or her property without a court order. A few hundred dollars can cost you a lot more in the long run. Avoid the temptation and do the right thing. Give the tenant his money back. And then drag him into court so you get paid. Some people may think this is too good to be true, but you will never regret doing the right thing.

82. I evicted a tenant who left her washer and dryer behind. A few days later she called and asked for the clothes inside the dryer. What should I do?

Give her everything she owns. It can be frustrating, but you don't want to wind up in court defending yourself against claims that you stole her clothes. If she owes you money, hire a collection agency to collect it (if it's worth the time and effort), but don't take things into your own hands. Take the high road and always do the right thing.

83. My tenant's car just got repossessed. She asked if I would come and pick up the rent because she doesn't have ride. Should I go get it?

No. If you do it one month for one tenant you soon be doing it every month for every tenant. It's her responsibility to get the rent to you. If she can't walk to a post office, she can have someone else take her. Use your energy and time to find the next big deal. Don't waste it by driving across town to pick up a check for a few hundred dollars.

84. My tenant's ten-year old son just fell out of a tree in the back-yard and broke his arm. The tenant just got the bill from the hospi-tal and asked if he could take it off the rent. He has the receipt but no insurance. What should I do?

Nothing. You don't have any responsibility to pay for accidents like this. When the tenant asks, be firm but fair. Paying for bumps and bruises and the occasional broken arm is part of being a parent. You didn't do anything wrong, and there is no reason you should have to foot the bill.

85. One of my tenants asked for me to come over and look at her leaking toilet. When I arrived, she was naked. What should I do?

Run. Do not pass go; do not collect $200. Get out of the room as quickly as possible. Of course, it's easy for me to say this because I have the most beautiful, supportive wife in the world, and I would never do anything to put our relationship at risk. Offers like this can be tempting, but if you ac-cept them you might as well kiss your empire goodbye. Owning real estate is an amazing opportunity to build wealth and to create financial freedom. Using it as a dating service is a guaranteed way to wind up in the poor house or jail. Don't risk everything for one night of pleasure.

86. My tenant believes the world is going to end and asked me to install a generator in case the power goes out. How do I handle this?

Tell him to adjust the tinfoil in his helmet and get a job if he wants the generator. You're not obligated to install one, even if your tenant thinks aliens are about to land. If you do buy into the conspiracy and get the generator, make sure you adjust his rent. You need to get your cash back before the zombies start knocking on your door.

87. My tenant is a college student who wants to go home during the summer. He asked if we would store his stuff in the garage and rent the house out until he returns. What should we do?

He needs to find a better storage place. Don't tie up one of your properties for several months to suit his needs. If he wants to pay the full rent for the summer months he can store his stuff wherever he wants. If not, he can find a storage unit in the yellow pages or online. Don't reduce your cash flow as a favor to him.

88. A perspective tenant has cash and is ready to rent today. Should I let them rent the property?

This is always a red flag, and you should avoid renting to pushy people who are in a hurry. It can be very tempting when people offer you a fist full of cash, but there is always a reason they need to rent in a hurry. Maybe they are trying to sign a lease with you before their current landlord files eviction papers. Or maybe one of them is about to lose his job. Whatever the reason, be leery when a prospect is willing to pay in cash on the spot and needs to move in today. If it looks too good to be true, it probably is.

89. A perspective tenant asked if we would hold a property for him because he has sixty days left on his current lease. He really wants our property. What should I do?

It's too early to rent to him. Another tenant may come in tomorrow and be ready to move in at the first of the month. If you get tied up with the first tenant, you just cost yourself two months' rent. Don't rush into a deal. If the property is still available in a month, the first tenant can come in and sign the lease. Don't mess with your cash flow by signing a deal to early. We will agree to hold property for fourteen days, but we never go any longer than that unless the prospective tenant pays the full rent to hold it.

90. Can I go on vacation if I own rental properties?

Yes. Owning property is very rewarding, but it can be demanding, too. You have to take care of yourself. Take time off to be with your family and re-charge your batteries. If you don't, you'll wind up getting burned out, and that won't be good for anyone. I can't tell you how many landlords I've met who never took any time off. Every one of them regretted it. But you have to have a plan when you are gone. Hire someone you trust to collect the rent, and make sure he can handle any problems that come up. Enjoy your time off and hit the ground running when you get back.

91. Should I carry a gun to collect rent?

Owning a weapon is a big responsibility. When you have a gun, a small dis-agreement can escalate into a felony murder charge in a few seconds. One bad decision can ruin lives forever. I know landlords who would never go collect rent without a gun. Their properties were in such rough areas it was the only way they felt comfortable. I think there is a bigger issue here. It is not your responsibility to go and collect rent. It is the tenant's responsibility to deliver rent. So if you have to get in your car, drive to your houses, and get your tenants to pay you, you need to change that dynamic as soon as possible. Meet with your tenants and tell then they need to mail their rent to you (make sure they give it enough time for it to be deliver by the due date) or they can drop it off at the office each month. Your time (and life) is too valuable to waste it by going out to collect rent.

92. Can I own a rental property in another state?

Absolutely. I know many investors who own property in several states. Don't limit your empire by buying in only one or two zip codes. Think big. If you do buy property in another state, make sure you understand the local laws and regulations. Laws vary from state to state, and just because you can do something in one place it doesn't mean you can do it in another. You might even consider buying in another country, if it meets your goals and fits into your portfolio.

93. Do I have to have my real estate license to manage my properties?

No. I don't have one, and neither do most of the investors I know. That's one of the great things about being an investor. You don't have to get any degrees or licenses. As long as you are able to finance the properties, you are good to go. I tried to get my license, but I didn't see what value it would add. I ended up dropping out after a few classes.

94. My tenant wants a phone line in the bedroom. Should I install it?

Do you hear that? It's the 1980s calling and it wants its corded phone back. No, you should not install a phone line into a certain room of the house. As long as there is a phone line connected to one jack in the house, you have met your obligation as a property manager. If your tenant wants a jack in a certain room, she can pay for it herself or pony up the cash for a cordless phone.

95. What happens to my real estate portfolio when I pass away?

It depends on how much estate planning you have done. If you don't do anything and die intestate (without a will) your heirs will have to pay for the estate to be probated. This means a judge will have to appoint an administrator, publish notice of the probate, and preside over several hearings before your assets are distributed. In most states, the probate process will take several months and cost thousands of dollars. You can avoid this by speaking to an attorney and doing some basic estate planning. This will allow you to speed up the process, save your heirs money, and ensure your property goes where you want it to go.

96. How much time does it take to be a real estate investor?

Being an investor can be a full-time job, but how you spend your time will change as you buy more and more properties. When you start, you will spend a lot of time finding properties (including inspecting and researching), negotiating deals, getting your financial statements in order so that you can get financing, and rehabbing, repairing, and maintaining your properties. But as your company grows, if you are savvy you will start hiring people to do most of those things. That will allow you to focus on putting together deals, and you will be able to buy more properties and better properties. Once you build your empire, you can put it on autopilot. You will have the right systems and people in place, and you will spend all your time cashing the checks.

97. What's the big hype about having an LLC when I only own one property?

It may not make sense to you to have an LLC when you first start, but there are two main reasons you should create one before you get your first property. First, an LLC will protect your assets in the event something goes wrong. If you get sued, the plaintiff and his lawyers shouldn't be able to touch any of the property owned by the LLC. Second, think big. You may only own one property today, but if you're savvy and diligent, you may own fifty or a hundred in a few years. If you start with good habits, it will make your life much easier as your empire grows. Plus, holding yourself out as the president of an LLC gives you instant credibility.

98. Should I have general liability insurance?

Yes. I can't imagine owning real estate without having enough insurance to protect me in the event someone claims they were injured on my property. Even a frivolous lawsuit can cost you more than the premiums on a basic policy. You should meet with an insurance agent who is experienced with real estate investors before you buy your first property. You have too much to lose to not have insurance.

99. When should I be self-insured on my properties?

You should be self-insured only when you can afford to lose all of your properties. What happens if a major storm, fire, or earthquake hits? Will you be able to survive if most or all of your income producing properties are damaged? Can you afford to have them rebuilt? These are the questions you need to ask if you start thinking about being self-insured.

100. One of my houses burned down and the tenant lost everything. What do I do?

Make sure that your tenant is safe. If he is not at the house, use the contact information on his application and let him know what happened. Your responsibilities are to make sure the property is secure and to call your insurance adjuster as quickly as possible. Hopefully, your tenant has renter's insurance and he can file a claim with his insurance company. If not, it may sound harsh, but it's not your problem. Your insurance covers your property and your property alone. Don't let your emotions take over and get sucked into paying for things when you are not obligated to. Keep a list of charities and organizations that will help your tenants after disasters, like the Red Cross and local churches.

101. How can I tell if damage is normal wear and tear?

After you have owned a few properties, you will develop an eye for what is "normal" wear and tear. It is normal for carpet to get worn down in high traffic areas, such as between the kitchen and the living room. It is not normal for the carpet to be covered with cigarette burns or oil stains. It is normal for a little dirt to accumulate where hands touch a door, such as near the doorknob. It is not normal to have holes in the wall caused by someone who became angry and punched the wall. And be sure to take pictures of the property before the tenant moves in and after he moves out. If there's a dispute about whether or not he is entitled to his deposit, it will be great to wave those in front of the judge. And remember, if the tenant broke it, it's not normal wear and tear.

102. What is the maximum number of people who can live in a two-bedroom home?

This can vary from place to place. Some cities and states have very strict guidelines on how many people can live in housing units, other places have no limits. You need to consult with your attorney and make sure that you understand what the local jurisdiction says. But here are a few thoughts. First, no one should be living in your property if you have not approved him or her. Tenants are not allowed to let anyone live with them without your permission. Second, regardless of what laws or ordnances allow, never let so many people on the property that they create a safety hazard. If it's legal for you to rent to thirteen people in one apartment and you want to try it, that's okay. But consider what will happen if there's an emergency and someone gets trampled as all of them try to make it out the door. Do you think you will get a call from an attorney trying to find the person with the deepest pockets? Be sure to review your insurance policy because it might limit the number of people you are allowed to have living in the property.

103. What is the difference between managing a single-family home and a multi-unit property?

In theory, there's not much difference. You own several different properties, there just located in one place. There are a few practical differences. The first is common areas. In a multi-unit, you have to spray for pests, maintain walkways, stairwells, and hallways, and you probably won't have to deal with things like that if you stick to single-family units. Another issue has to do with utilities. Handling utilities in single-family units is simple. There is one meter for the gas, one meter for the electricity, and one water bill. In a multi-unit, you need to make sure each unit has its own meter for gas and electricity and that each one is billed separately for the trash pickup and water. If not, you may be responsible for all of these bills. Trust me. You do not want to learn that the hard way like I did.

104. What do I do if someone is severely injured on the property?

The first thing you need to do is to make sure to call 911. You need to get the person medical attention as quickly as possible. Then you need to call your insurance agent and tell him what happened. He may send an adjuster to the property to do an investigation and find out why the injury happened and if you need to make any changes to the property. Don't ever hide anything or lie about what you know. You may think you are making things better by secretly fixing a broken step or clearing ice from the sidewalk, but you aren't. If things ever go to court, it may make you look guilty. And if you look guilty, it may cost you a lot of money. Document everything. When money is on the line, some people have a habit of misremembering things. You'll be surprised at how quickly a tenant's story can change when he thinks he is going to get a big check from your insurance company, and you don't want to foot the bill if you didn't do anything wrong.

105. Things have been going badly, and I don't have money for repairs, taxes, or mortgage payments. What now?

Being short of cash is a killer when you are a real estate investor. You are going to have difficult months, and you need to prepare by having an emergency fund. I recommend setting aside six months of insurance payments, mortgage payments, and taxes for each property. If you haven't done that (or if you have burned through it already), it may be time to consider temporarily downsizing. It would be better to sell off a few properties when you still have equity than to do nothing and watch the properties deteriorate or to have tax liens put on them. The worst option would be to owe a mortgage and back taxes on property that is in such bad shape it has to be torn down. That may destroy your ability to build an empire.

106. The tenant painted the walls ugly colors and now I have to repaint. Do I charge her?

Absolutely. Charge her for every drop of paint, the drop cloths, and the cost of hiring someone to paint them. You need to have the property in rent-ready condition before you show it to prospects, and not everyone is going to be excited about eating breakfast in a pea green dining room.

107. Suddenly half my properties are vacant and my mortgage payments are eating me alive. What do I do?

You have to find more tenants. I'm not trying to be a smart aleck, but that's the only way you're going to get your cash flow back to where it needs to be. You have to get qualified people to move into your units. Get off your butt, hit the pavement, and find some new tenants. If you've done everything you can and you still have empty properties, it might be time to consider unloading some of them or refinancing your loans. These should only be done as a last resort. You want to keep your credit open so that you can buy more properties, and if you tie up your financing because you didn't plan for rough patches, your business won't grow as fast as it should.

108. What is the best way to find tenants?

If you don't have a steady stream of renters, you might as well close up shop. You need to attract new tenants like your life depends on it, because it does. There are a lot of ways to get new tenants. You can put up a sign in the front yard of your vacant properties, place ads on websites like Craigslist, and use the classifieds in newspapers and fliers available at the supermarket. Tell your friends and family that you need to find tenants. Be sure to talk to the people who live near your houses. They can be a great asset as many of them may have friends they want to live near. It's important to not be passive when you need tenants. Take action. Your tenants won't just accidently find their way to your properties. It's going to take action and focus on your part.

109. My tenants keep harassing and bothering the neighbors. How do I handle this?

You need to take care of this as quickly as possible. Your neighbors may live next to your property longer than your tenant will rent from you, and you want to keep them on your side. Make sure you document everything. Send your tenant a letter stating what the neighbor has told you, and ask for his side of the story in writing. You want to be sure to investigate the situation. Even if you know that the neighbor is telling the truth, you need to document the fact that you did your due diligence. If you have to take the tenant to court, you need to be able to show the judge how you did everything you could to before you took legal action. If the tenant doesn't start behaving better (or at least leaving people alone), then you will need to start the process of getting rid of him. Hopefully, you will be near the end of your lease and can simply refuse to renew it. If not, you'll have to start the eviction process. When you visit with your attorney to draft your lease, make sure you address this issue. The last thing you want is to be struck with a lousy tenant you can't evict when you could have avoided the problem with one simple clause.

110. There was a meth lab in my property. How do I legally make it rentable?

If one of your properties has been used as a meth lab notify your local law enforcement agency immediately. Meth is a potent drug, and the only way people can make it is with caustic chemicals, such as brake fluid, batteries, and fertilizer. People who cook meth aren't concerned with disposing of these things in a responsible manner, so the houses they use as labs will wind up with piles of these dangerous chemicals. Plus, during the process, deadly gases can be released and these gasses soak into the walls and floors and can even make their way to your neighbors' houses. These gases can cause lung, skin, and eye problems, so you have to take the situation very seriously. After the police have been notified, they will most likely bring in a hazardous materials unit to take out all the chemicals and the tools used to make meth, and you will be responsible for making sure the property is safe enough to rent to tenants. But just airing out the property and slapping on fresh coat of paint probably won't be enough. You will have to clean the vents, the plumbing, replace any carpet, and every surface in the house will have to be thoroughly scrubbed. It's a good idea to hire a professional cleaning company that specializes and has experience in handling these types of messes. The stakes are high and you don't want to pinch pennies when it comes cleaning up a former meth lab. Be sure to keep copies of your receipts for your tax records.

111. My tenant wants to buy the property. How does "rent to own" work?

If you don't learn anything else from this book, learn this: do rent to own whenever you can. Grab the down payment, get the tenant under contract, and smile all the way to the bank. Using rent to own can be a great way to build your empire. The short version is that the buyer and seller agree that the buyer will lease the property for a certain amount of time (such as three to five years), and after that he has the option to purchase the property. It can be a great way for people with bad credit to finance a property. And as a seller, it's a good way to maximize your cash flow. One of the interesting things about rent to owns is that most of them never get completed, and you may wind up selling the same property several times.

112. My tenant treats the property well and pays on time. But she calls me twelve times a month to ask questions and ask for upgrades and repairs. She's driving me nuts. How do I handle this?

Tenants like this are a real pain in the butt. The good part is you don't have to worry about getting paid each month, but the downside is that they monopolize so much of your time and energy you wonder if it worth being a landlord. They remind me of something I was told, called "The Cost of Making Money." What this means is that in every job you have to do certain things to make money. When you are not being paid enough to do those things, it may be time to reevaluate your career, or to at least to change how you do things. Part of owning investment real estate is dealing with tenants, and sometimes they can be demanding. When you have one who is making unreasonable demands on your time, you need to ask yourself if she is worth it. Is the security of having her rent check every month worth more than the pain she causes? If the answer is no, let her lease run out and rent the property to someone else as quickly as you can.

113. Should I let my tenants know where I live?

Never. If you let your tenants know where you live, you will never get a moment's rest. When something goes wrong, some of them will drive over to your house and knock on your door at 3:00 in the morning to "encourage" you to fix it right then and there. They won't bother calling the office or the handyman. They'll just show up with a frown and an attitude. Plus, you will eventually have to evict someone, and a few of those people have been known to carry grudges. Do you really want them to know where you live? Never give out your address and you will sleep easier at night.

114. What happens to my real estate portfolio if I get divorced?

I hope you never have to go through a divorce. It costs money and ruins lives. But the unfortunate truth is that some of you will get divorced. Marriage is an important institution, and when one ends it is traumatic and expensive. A few sheets of paper filed at the courthouse can destroy the business it took you years to build. If you are married, make sure you give your family the time, love, and support it deserves. Your business is important, but it will never be as important as your wife and children. If you're not married, use this opportunity to plan your business so you can survive a divorce if you have to endure one in the future. Property division comes down to several important factors: where you live, when you bought the property, and how much you plan. This, of course, is only a guide, and you will need to consult with your attorney to get the specifics for your area. States fall into one of two types of property division during a divorce. Community property states (where all assets acquired during the marriage are divided equally), and equitable division (where property acquired during the marriage is divided according to rules designed to make it seem more fair). The general rule is: If you bought property during the course of the marriage, your spouse may make a claim on it during the divorce. If you bought it before the marriage, it's yours to keep. So if you are thinking about buying more property and you just got engaged, it might be a good idea to go ahead and get the deal done before you exchange your vows. That will probably make the investment a "premarital asset," and it is yours to keep.

115. How often should I use an exterminator?

Exterminate a home whenever you see pests, but set off a few bug bombs before you bring in the professionals. They may look small, but some bugs (such as termites) can destroy a home. When you see a few of them, you can bet there are thousands more you don't. You might also be forced to exterminate whenever a tenant moves out and leaves the place in shambles. If a tenant hasn't cared for the property like he should have, bugs and other pests can flock to your property. If you inspect a property after evicting a tenant and cockroaches flee when you turn on the kitchen light, get the property exterminated. Of course, you can also become a licensed exterminator and save a bunch of money by doing it yourself.

116. The tenant is paying rent, but not utilities. He's living with no heat or electricity. What now?

He either needs to get with the program and have the utilities turned on or he needs to move out. You own the property and you need to protect it, and that means having heat in the wintertime to make sure the pipes don't burst. If your tenant wants to live off the grid he needs to buy his own place where he can do whatever he pleases.

117. I just visited my property, and the place is very dirty and messy. Should I make the tenant clean it up? How?

Yes. Part of the responsibility of being a tenant is keeping the property clean and habitable. Notify her in writing that the apartment needs to be cleaned and give her a deadline. Be sure to inspect the property immediately after the deadline, and if it's still not clean notify her that she is in breach of her lease.

118. My tenant's ex-boyfriend keeps cruising past the house and stalking her. Is this my problem?

This is a very fine line. The last thing you want to do is to get caught up in someone else's domestic drama. Your job is to provide habitable housing, and you must maintain a professional business relationship with your tenants that may sometimes mean keeping distance although this may appear that you do not care. If you know one of your tenants is having a domestic situation; you might refer them to a local support group for women in abusive relationships. Never offer to undertake anything more than that, such as sitting in your car at night with a baseball bat just in case the guy drives buy. Things like that never end well.

119. My tenant was in a terrible accident and can't walk or get out of bed. She can't work or pay rent. How can I kick her out on the street?

Slow your roll, Dr. Evil. Yes, this business is all about cash flow, and there will be times when you have to evict people. But you need to temper that with a little compassion. If you read The Savvy Landlord, you know I had to evict a woman who was a terrible hoarder. She had accumulated so much trash it was a serious fire hazard. But I knew she had issues and I paid for my assistant to find her a new place to live. The tenant had issues, and I didn't want to just throw her out on the street. If your tenant was paying her rent on time and the only issue is the injury, you might want to go the extra mile and make sure she has a place to live with family, friends, or with a church or other charitable organization before you force her out. Plus, how will it look if one of the local TV stations shows up with a crew demanding to know why you are such a heartless jerk? In this situation, it would probably be worth a few hundred dollars of uncollected rent to do the right thing.

120. My property taxes just went up $50 a month. How much should I raise the rent?

You won't be able to do anything until the lease is up. And even then, you will need to make sure you can justify the increase. Will your rent still be competitive with the increase? Will you be stepping over dollars to get to pennies? Before you do anything, make sure you crunch the numbers and that they work in your favor.

121. After I filed a claim on my roof, my insurance company dropped me and nobody wants to insure the property. What now?

I've been through this, and I know how frustrating it is. It may take you awhile, but you will be able to find a company to insure your property. You just have to stay focused and contact as many companies as you can. And it may even work to your advantage if you find a company that insures you and gives you a better rate or increases your policy limits.

122. I couldn't sleep last night, and as I was channel surfing at 3:30 in the morning, I watched an infomercial about real estate investing. They made it look really easy. I did a quick internet search about managing property, and I think I'm ready to start buying. Real estate investing will give me the chance to be a multi-millionaire by the end of the month, right?

Put down the Red Bull and take a breath. Real estate investing is a great opportunity, and it will give you a lifestyle most people will only dream of. But your success will be determined by your hard work and willingness to learn from others and from your mistakes. It is not a "get rich quick" scheme. It takes a lot of sweat and hard work, and anyone who tells you otherwise doesn't know what he is talking about. But if you are willing to put in the work, you will reap rewards and can make a lot of money.

123. The tenant has disappeared but his stuff is still in the house. How long do I have to wait before I get rid of it?

You need to file the paperwork and start the eviction process (assuming his lease is not up). If you rush right out and throw everything in the trash, you can bet he will say you threw away the original Picasso his grandmother gave him. Take it slow, do it by the book, and save yourself the headache.

124. I suspect my tenant is an illegal alien. Should I do something?

This is a hot topic right now. Some communities have passed ordinances and laws requiring landlords to confirm whether or not tenants are in the country legally. If you live in one of those areas (check with your attorney if you are not sure), you obviously have to comply with the law. But if not, I wouldn't do anything. "Suspecting" is a long way from knowing, and you don't want to waste your time defending yourself against false allegations that you discriminate against people who don't look like you. The law will sort this out over time, and when that happens you will know what to do.

125. I have the best tenant in the world, but she's fallen on hard times. She is asking me to reduce the rent so she doesn't have to move. Should I?

How much of a deduction does she need? Are we talking 10 percent a month? Or is it 50 percent? There is a lot of value in having good tenants in your properties, and if it were only a few dollars a month I would consider it. But there is a point where it would be smarter to get a new tenant, and that would depend on how much she needs.

126. My rental property has doubled in value. Should I sell and take the profit, or hold and keep the cash flow?

Congratulations on being such a savvy landlord and buying a sweet property. Never sell a property unless you know what you are going to do with the money. Will you put it into more properties? Also, never sell a property just because you received a good offer. Only sell if selling fits your overall investment strategy. If you can't explain why it is good to sell the property, hold onto it and keep cashing the rent checks.

127. All my properties are in a town that just passed restrictive rules on landlords. My life is suddenly hell, and I can't sell because nobody wants to buy rentals here anymore. Am I screwed?

Let's start by saying the town didn't do you any favors. The city just re-crunched your numbers and didn't even have the courtesy to check with you first. Hopefully, you have enough in your emergency fund to buy you some time before you have to make a decision. If enough investors are impacted, you might consider meeting with the city council to try and get some relief. If worst comes to worst, you'll need an exit strategy. Put the properties on the market. Someone will buy your property, regardless of how badly the city shafted you. It's just a matter of waiting it out and finding the right price.

128. I bought a house with no money down from another investor, and it's not working out. Nobody wants to rent or buy the house. Should I just walk away from the property and the loan?

This is another example of why your property should be in an LLC or corporation. If you have to walk away, the company is responsible and not you. You never want to pull up stakes and just run away, but sometimes you don't have any other choices. You will face setbacks as you build your portfolio, and you can't take them personally. If you can't find a way to make the deal work, the most responsible thing to do may be to meet with the seller and tell him you have to give the property back. Most investors will understand this, and some of them will even be grateful, because it means they can resell the property. I had to return several properties when I was building my portfolio. It wasn't easy, but I learned from the experience, and I'm in a better position today because I went through that.

129. I am a successful man, and I want to invest my money. I've never been a landlord, but I have the opportunity to buy a killer "package deal" of forty properties from a retiring investor. Is this a good idea?

You have to crawl before you can walk, and it sounds like you are trying to run the Boston Marathon before you put on your first pair of shoes. This is one of the most common mistake new investors make. They buy too many properties too quickly. It almost never works out well. Start with one or two, make sure you understand what it takes to be an investor, and then jump in the deep end. Your success in one area won't necessarily translate to success in investing, so be sure you have one or two properties under your belt before you buy a big package deal. Relax. More deals will follow if you stay in the game.

130. How do I find a good handyman?

The best way is to ask other investors if there is someone they would rec-ommend. But the problem is that good help is so hard to find, and no one wants to lose good handymen. You can also place ads on websites like Craigslist, and interview the people who respond. When you find a good one, take care of him. Pay him on time and let him know he is appreciated. Trust me. It will be worth it in the long run.

131. Is it worth it to replace all the windows and insulation to make the house more energy efficient?

Only if you are able to pass the expenses off to your tenants by raising the rent to pay for the upgrade. For some people, energy efficiency is a big issue. They want to save money on utilities and are concerned about the environment. For other tenants, all they care about is the monthly rent. So if you make the upgrade, you will have to be sure to find tenants who will understand the value of energy efficiency.

132. I am considering the purchase of a rental house. It's in a rural area and has a well and septic tank. Should I be concerned?

No. Wells and septic tanks are nothing to be concerned about, but you have to understand how they work and what the costs will be. You don't want to buy the property unless you understand how the maintenance will impact your cash flow. You also need to be armed with information in the event you have to call someone out to fix one of them. If you have no working knowledge and one of them breaks, you will be at the mercy of the person you call for repairs. And that is not the position you want to be in.

133. I'm considering buying a vacation rental that rents out by the week. Are these good investments?

They can be. Be sure to ask for copies of the seller's records, including rental contracts, bank deposits, and receipts for any repairs. If he tells you the property rents out for most of the year, he should be able to document that fairly easily. If he can't, he may be inflating the value of the property and hoping your greed will get the best of you. Regardless of how good a deal sounds, always verify what the seller is telling you. Also consider how you will manage the property, if it is not near where you live.

134. The last time I went to collect the rent the tenant was drunk and acted threatening. I'm afraid to go back there. What should I do?

Get rid of this guy as quickly as you can for two reasons. First, why do you have to go collect the rent? His job is to pay you. It is not your job to find him and beg to be paid. If he's not willing to address an envelope, put a stamp on it, and drop it in a mailbox, he needs to live somewhere else.

Second, if he displays that type of aggression over paying his rent (which he voluntarily agreed to do), it's only a matter of time before he explodes over something else and does more than threaten people. Get rid of him as quickly as you can.

135. The tenant always disappears around the first of the month. I'm tired of tracking him down for the rent. What now?

Quit looking for him. One of two things will happen. He will either pay his rent on time (which is what you want) or he will not (which means serving the tenant, with the paperwork, starting the eviction process). The reason you have to track him down each month is because you have a dysfunctional landlord-tenant relationship, and you're enabling him. He doesn't understand what his obligations are or is unwilling to live up to them. It takes two to continue that pattern, and if you keep looking for him it's not going to get any better. Don't waste your valuable time by playing this game anymore. If you still have this problem six months from now, you have no one to blame but yourself.

136. Whenever I drive by a property, my tenant has a bunch of shady-looking "friends" hanging out on the porch and the front lawn. How do I get rid of them?

This is a very touchy area. It drives me crazy when I look at one of my properties and I know that my tenant has brought the wrong kind of people into the neighborhood. It's only a matter of time before I start having more problems with him and his buddies. When I see this happen, I start finding creative ways to encourage my tenant to move. Are there any cars parked in the yard? If so, I make an anonymous call to the code enforcement unit and hope they show up and ticket him. And I encourage my friends and family to drive by the property and do the same anytime they see a code violation. If the tenant needs anything from me, you can believe it won't be done quickly. I always find something better to do than to than to rush over and take care of him. I do the absolute minimum to honor the lease and protect my property. If he is late on his rent, I send him a Notice to Quit, and when the lease is up, I start looking for another tenant.

137. I want to invest in real estate, but Dave Ramsay says not to go into debt. It would take forever to save enough cash. What should I do?

I agree with Dave when he is talking about consumer debt. It's not a good idea to owe thousands of dollars on credit cards because you had to get a new pair of custom-made ostrich-skin cowboy boots but you couldn't afford to pay cash. But borrowing money to buy real estate is different. The only way real estate investors accumulate wealth is by leveraging their money. And that means borrowing other people's money. If you won't do that, you will never get on the fast lane, and your business will wither and die. You will also be entitled to a bunch of tax deductions when you borrow money to buy properties. Of course, you have to keep the debt manageable, make good business decisions, and plan for rough times. If you are serious about building an empire, you will have to borrow money to do it.

138. Should I base my values on the information at zillow.com?

When you are trying to determine the value of your property, it's important to have as much information as possible, and that includes researching sites such as zillow.com. But they shouldn't be your only source of information. The most important way you will know the true value of your property is experience. When you truly understand your market, you will know what is a fair rental or sale price. When you see a property for sale or rent in your area, ask what the rental or sales price is. After a while, you will know if your prices are fair and you won't spend too much or charge too little.

139. Real estate is a long-term investment. How can I make money right now?

You should always look at your properties as a long-term investment, but there are times when you need to make money quickly. One of the best ways is flipping. Flipping happens when you buy a property, make a few improvements, and sell it for a quick profit. It's not uncommon for people to make more than $10,000 a few months after buying a property. You can also get "birddog" fees by finding properties and referring them to other investors. Another option is wholesaling, which means you get property under contract and then sell it to another investor for a profit. It's a great way to make quick money without putting any cash in the deal. But substantial, long-term wealth will only come from owning and renting property.

140. What deductions and allowances can I take when tax time rolls around?

Many of the deductions allowed in our tax code were created for property owners, and this is one of the best reasons to own investment property. The list is too long to include it here (and it changes every year), so be sure to consult with your accountant. A few of the highlights are the interest on your mortgage, payroll taxes, office equipment, and salaries. Make sure you take every deduction you are legally entitled to take. If not, you are throwing money away.

141. Does my spouse have to be at the closing?

Only if her name will appear on the title. If you have planned properly, any property you buy will be placed in a business structure (such as an LLC or corporation), and only the president needs to sign for it.

142. What is a HUD form?

The HUD, or HUD-1, is a form used at closings. It's also called a settlement or closing statement, and the HUD stands for "Housing and Urban Development." It lists all the expenses each party has to pay. You are entitled to receive a copy of one the day before your actual closing. Be sure to examine this carefully before you sign it. If there is anything you don't understand or if there are charges you didn't expect to see, make sure you ask about them. The closing isn't final until you sign off on it, and you can negotiate any terms that you haven't seen before.

143. Why are closing costs so high?

Let me be perfectly clear. Closing costs are a complete and total rip off. They exist solely so that title companies and banks can make money. They charge them because the law allows them to do it and because they know homeowners and investors will pay them. I've looked at this issue, and that's really the best answer I can come up with. There is no reason why they have to be so expensive, other than the fact that people keep paying them. If a candidate would run for office with a platform of outlawing closing costs, he would have my vote.

144. What does PMI mean?

PMI stands for private mortgage insurance, and it's another rip off. Some private lenders will require you to purchase this in case you default on the mortgage. It insures the bank if you default on your loan. You will make the payment as part of your mortgage each month. But here's the part that pisses me off. They have already done a review of your credit history and approved your loan. Plus, you are being charged interest on your mortgage, and that rate is based on your creditworthiness. And, you're only charged PMI if you owe more than 80 percent of the value of the property. For example, if you bought a $100,000 dollar house with $15,000 down, you would have to pay PMI. But, when you owe less than 20 percent of the value of the property, the PMI doesn't automatically go away. You still have to pay it, even when the bank is virtually guaranteed of getting its money back if you default. The only way to get rid of PMI is to make a request to your lender. They will require an appraisal to see how much equity you have, which you will have to pay for. So make sure you crunch the numbers and see if getting rid of PMI will save you any money.

145. Can I get a second loan for the down payment?

You can finance the down payment on some FSBOs, but you will probably have a hard time financing the down payment with a traditional lender such as a bank. Banks have become much more cautious during the last few years, and they expect you to have a sizable down payment in cash. Some banks won't finance deals if you don't have at least 70 percent LTV. I financed a down payment on a property when I was getting started, but I haven't done that in a while.

146. I have the keys to my new property, but I haven't closed on it yet. Should I wait until after the closing to start working on it?

Yes, that is the best way to do things. No deal is done until the closing is finished, and you don't want to put time and money into a property only to have the deal yanked out from beneath you at the last minute. If that happens, you won't have any way to recover your investment in the property. I once installed a new bathroom floor in a property before it closed. It was a risk, but it was a HUD deal and I felt confident everything would work out. Fortunately, the deal closed and I started cash flowing on the house.

147. An investor asked me to make the earnest money check payable to him. Should I do that?

No. Never make an earnest check out to an investor. Always make it out to the title company. I did that once, and instead of using the money as a down payment on the property; the investor spent it on himself. I got screwed out of the money. Protect your business and only pay earnest money to a reputable title company.

148. When making offers should I make a formal offer, a letter of intent, or a verbal offer?

You will probably use all three. Almost every deal will start with a verbal offer. You will find a property you like, negotiate with the seller or his agent in person or over the phone, and agree on a price. But that doesn't mean anything. Verbal offers aren't worth the paper they are written on, so you will need to follow up your conversations with a formal offer as quickly as possible. The longer you wait, the more likely the other party is going to have buyer's/seller's remorse, so get this done before he changes his mind. A letter of intent is a great way to find out if the owner of the property is interested in selling a property that is not on the market. A letter of intent is a non-binding offer that includes all the major points, such as selling price, the down payment, and whether or not the seller would carry financing (and if so the length and interest rate). It's a great way to inquire about property that you are interested in, even if you don't see a For Sale sign on the property. If you use a letter of intent, make sure your offer is reasonable. There's nothing wrong with trying to negotiate a good deal, but if you lowball the owner you won't be taken seriously and you may not be able to build a relationship that would help you get more deals in the future.

149. How do I get a proof of funds letter?

A proof of funds letter is a statement from your bank demonstrating the fact that you have the ability to pay for a property. Some savvy investors won't deal with buyers who cannot demonstrate they have the ability to pay for a property (especially if it is worth more than $50,000), because it is a complete waste of time to spend weeks negotiating on a property only to find out the buyer can't pay for it. The proof of funds separates the wheat from the chaff and prequalifies buyers. If you are a seller and are relying on proof of funds, be careful because it is not uncommon for con artists to use fraudulent ones. So always verify with the bank that the proof of funds is real. If you need to get one, visit with your banker. She should have no trouble documenting your ability to pay for the property and can issue a valid statement for you.

150. A tenant asked me if I would be willing to give him a discount if he stopped paying his rent late. What should I do?

Encourage him to honor his commitments by paying on time. If that doesn't work, there is one trick I have learned that works well for some people. I give some tenants a discount if they pay the rent early. If they don't pay it early, then they have to pay the entire amount on the due date. For example, if I need to clear $600 a month on a property, I draft the lease for $650, but then agree to charge the tenant $600 if he pays on or before the first. Some landlords charge late fees if the rent is not paid on time, but this can be tricky because some states have enacted laws to prevent excessively high fees, so make sure you understand what you are allowed to do in your area. I don't offer much of a discount (maybe 5 percent), and I've only done it with tenants who have been good tenants for a fairly long time. It is cheaper than putting time and energy into finding a new tenant, and it gets me around and laws regarding late fees.

151. A tenant wants to change the locks on her house. Should I let her?

No. No one should ever change a lock on your property except you. If the tenant wants to pay for you to change the locks, that's great. But you should never be in a situation where you don't have total control over who has access to your property. And if she changes the locks, that means you can't get into your property when you need to.

152. I just found out that my tenant changed the locks on the property. How do I handle this?

Get your handyman out to the property as quickly as possible, change the locks immediately, and follow up with a letter documenting what the tenant did and that it was a breach of the lease. This is no laughing matter. When you look at one of your properties, you shouldn't see bricks and mortar. You should see a big pile of your cash. You're the owner, and that house represents your financial security and how you will feed your family each month. When a tenant changes the locks, they have put bars around your money and taken control from you. You need to get this control back and make sure it never happens again.

153. What should I say or do when a perspective tenant explains he can get a co-signer before I even look at his application?

This is a red flag. What the tenant is really telling you is, "There is a problem with my credit. After you look at it, you probably won't want to rent to me." Ask the tenant if there are problems with his credit, and then run the application anyway. Many people have gone through tough times, such as a divorce or health problems, that have caused them to miss a payment or two. It's human nature for us to be hard on ourselves, and the prospect's credit may not be as bad as he thinks it is. When you run the report, you'll at least know what you are dealing with. Hopefully, it won't be that bad. If it is, you can still rent to him as long as you find a creditworthy co-signer.

154. What is the meaning of real estate?

Why does the sun rise and set? What is your purpose in the universe? Real estate means different things to different people. For some, it means the real property or brick and mortar they see when they look at a house. But for me it means a lot more, and it should mean more to you if you're an investor, too. To me, real estate is freedom. It's a way I can control my destiny and provide for my family's future. It's the way I build my empire and how I am going to make a positive impact in the world. People who look at real estate and only see a place to live need to improve their vision.

155. What is the difference between a real estate agent and a broker?

The short version is that a broker is the person who owns a real estate agency, and the agents are the people who work for him. Agents and brokers can both sell property, and both have to be licensed, but brokers have to get more training and have a different licensing process. Of course, agents pay a portion of their commissions to their brokers.

156. What is an REO?

In addition to being an awesome rock band from the 1970s, REO is an acronym for "real estate owned." It refers to property that has been foreclosed on and is owned by the lender. These three letters can mean a lot of money to you, because (as we have seen in the past few years), when banks foreclose on properties, they may be willing to cut some sweet deals. With an REO, they have the worst possible situation. They own an unoccupied property that they have to maintain and pay taxes on, but it is not generating any income. They can be desperate to get those properties off their books as soon as possible. So keep your eyes out for REOs, because they can be a great way to buy property at a discount.

157. What is the difference between a full-blown appraisal and a drive-by appraisal?

There is a huge difference between these kinds of appraisals. A drive-by appraisal is one that is based on the exterior of the house and basic comps. You have to disclose the fact that an appraisal is a drive-by to your lenders, and you normally only do those when you don't have access to the inside of the house. You might do a drive-by if the owners are going through a difficult divorce or if the owner died and the property has not been probated yet. A full appraisal includes a detailed inspection of the interior of the home. Your bank will tell you which appraisal it needs.

158. What is the MLS? Do I have access to it?

The MLS is the Multiple Listing Service, a database of all the properties listed by Realtors in your area. Only licensed Realtors have access to it, so this is another reason to have a good working relationship with at least one Realtor. A Realtor can search by zip code, price range, and square footage to quickly find properties that you would be interested in. This can save you time and money when you are building your empire.

159. Should I get my real estate license so I can access the MLS?

This is more trouble than it is worth if you are serious about being an investor. There is nothing wrong with being licensed, but you don't need one to buy property. Plus, if you do get your license you'll have to complete a certain number of hours of continuing classes each year to keep the license. This is not a savvy way to spend your time. A better way to access the MLS is to develop a relationship with one or two Realtors. Let them do the legwork of going through the MLS to see if there are any great deals. Spend your time finding deals that will make you thousands, if not millions, of dollars instead of sitting in a classroom listening to someone drone on about real estate. Your time is your most valuable asset. Spend it wisely.

160. Can I find deals not listed on the MLS?

Absolutely. In fact, most of the deals you find will never be on the MLS. You'll be dealing with other investors who don't want to pay Realtor commissions, families who want or need to unload properties quickly, and banks or other institutions that own foreclosed properties they want to get rid of. Most of these properties will never be listed with a Realtor. In fact, if most of the properties you buy are on the MLS, you are probably paying too much for them. If you get out and hustle you can build a huge empire without using the MLS at all.

161. How much can I deduct from a security deposit?

You can deduct for any reasonable costs needed to get the property rent-ready (above normal wear and tear), and for any rent the tenant owes. This varies from state to state, so be sure you understand the laws in your area. In some states, you even have to place the deposit in a special bank account and provide an accounting for any money you don't return. Security deposits are there to protect you and your investments; they are not another revenue stream. Never take money out of a deposit without a valid reason for doing so.

162. My tenant damaged the property, and it's going to cost more than his security deposit to repair it. What can I do?

Start by documenting the damage. Take pictures and send the tenant a written list of what needs to be done. Then have every repair made, use his security deposit to pay for it, and bill him for the difference. Period. Don't wait until he pays you to have the repairs made, because he may refuse to pay you or dispute the charges, and then you'll be left with property that can't be rented. It's his responsibility to pay for the damage above normal wear and tear, and if he isn't willing to do that take him to court. If he still isn't willing to pay, turn the judgment over to a collection agency. And don't lose one minute of sleep over it. It's business. You're not the one who trashed the property.

163. How much can you increase the rent every year?

As much as you can get away with, as long you sign a new lease. But be careful about raising the rent too often. If you get greedy, you will live to regret it. Some tenants will be offended if you raise the rent every year, even if it is a small amount. At a certain point, they will think it is cheaper to move than to pay the increase. And you should always be able to justify any increase in rent. You can avoid situations where you have to frequently raise the rent by understanding your market and charging a rent that is fair at the start of each lease.

164. What's a hard money lender?

A hard money lender loans money based on the value of the property being mortgaged, and not the creditworthiness of the borrower. Other lenders typically look at the credit history of the borrower to determine if they are likely to get paid. Hard money lenders have no risk, because the entire value of their loans is backed by the equity in the property. In fact, if the borrower doesn't have a substantial amount of equity, hard money lenders probably won't do the deal. Hard money lenders can be a great source for bridge loans and for homeowners who have credit problems.

165. How do you know you are working with a good Realtor?

Pull out your bank statements and look at how much money she has made you. That's really what it comes down to. Your Realtor may be a nice lady, but if she isn't helping build your empire, you need to find someone else to do business with. Don't spend your time dealing with Realtors who don't understand your goals or share your passion for putting deals together. Make sure they call you back in a timely manner and share leads with you.

It's a red flag if they seem lazy when it comes time to put in an offer or if they have a good talk but don't get things done. Dealing with people who act this way is like trying to teach a pig to sing. You'll only waste your time and annoy the pig.

166. Do I need a real estate agent to buy property?

No. You can find your own properties, negotiate the deals, and even draft the contracts by yourself. But there is value in working with the right agent. Agents only get paid if you buy a property they send your way, so there is an incentive for them (and little risk for you) to hustle and bring you properties that fit into your goals and portfolio. A good agent is like an employee who works for free until she puts money in your pocket. An agent who understands your plans and the needs of investors is worth her weight in gold and will bring you deals you may not be able to find on your own.

167. How do I know how much a house is worth?

A house is worth whatever someone is willing to pay for it, just like a car, hockey skates, or jewelry. The only way to know the true value of a property is to really understand your market. How much do similar houses in the same neighborhood sell for? Does your property have more square footage or fewer bedrooms than the houses that have sold in the area recently? You can use the Internet and research the sales prices of comparable houses (or "comps") of houses that have sold recently. You might be able to find appraisals of other houses online as well. But the most important way to understand this is through experience. Once you start putting deals together, you'll understand what properties are really worth. And always consult with your mentor. Your mentor has travelled this road before and can make sure you are not overpaying for (or underselling) your property.

168. I'm crunching the numbers on my first deal and need to find out what the property taxes are. How do I find this information?

Congrats on starting on the right foot. You need to make money from day one, and you have to have as much information as possible to do that. You can find the property tax information at the county assessor's office. Most of this information is online now, and with just a few clicks of your mouse you can find the tax information for any address you want. Always factor in property taxes into your ROI or cash flow plan. If the deal is too skinny, wait for the next one.

169. Can I find out how much the owner paid for the property?

Yes. Again, this information is available at the county assessor's office, and can probably be found online. It's great to have this information when you are negotiating the price of a property, because you'll know exactly what the seller paid for the house and you'll know what you can offer so that he makes a fair profit. If he's not willing to take that, you can walk away. I wish I had done this when I started. I had a deal or two early in my career where I got cocky and thought I made great deals. After the closing was done I found out what the sellers had paid and was stunned to realize how much profit they made from me. I was a complete newbie and looking back I paid more than I should have. Learn from my mistake and get as much information as you can before you spend your hard-earned cash.

170. How do I analyze a deal and know it's going to cash flow before I buy the property?

The simple answer is to know how much it's going to cost and how much you can rent it for. If you can pay all the bills and have money left over, you have positive cash flow. The trick is to understand the real cost of ownership and to know what properties rent for in your market. The real cost of ownership isn't just the mortgage payment. It also includes insurance, property taxes, the cost of repairing or rehabbing the property to make it rent ready, and any holding or maintenance costs. You will only know what properties rent for in your market by researching the area and renting a property or two. Whenever I analyze a deal, I use a simple spreadsheet called a pro forma. I create a column and at the top I put the rent I can expect to charge. Beneath that I subtract all of my expenses. If I cash flow at least $100 a month I will probably do the deal. If I hit $200, I will definitely do it, and if I squeeze $300 I'll do it and party like a rock star.

171. Should I invest in single-family units or multi-family units?

You can make money in both, but you have to know what you are doing. In The Savvy Landlord, I devote an entire section of the book to interviewing other landlords, and I asked almost every one of them this question. Most people start in single-family because that is what they are familiar with. We understand that people will always need places to live, and when most of us think about that we see houses. I started with single-family, then branched out to multi-family, and bought my first apartment a year ago. You need to invest in whichever area you feel comfortable, and then work your butt of to be successful.

172. What is escrow?

Escrow is a service used by buyers and sellers to make sure all the parties do what they say they will do. When a buyer puts his funds in escrow, it means he has deposited the money in an account controlled by an escrow agent. Both parties have a say in choosing this person or institution, and they also agree on written instructions about how and when the money will be transferred. The money is not transferred until the closing. The benefit is that the seller knows that the buyer is serious about purchasing the property and has the money to make it happen. It's great for the buyer because he doesn't lose control of the money until title is transferred. Escrow eliminates the risk people feel when they "go first" in a deal and hope the others follow them.

173. How do I handle a closing without a real estate agent?

If you do your deals by yourself (which I recommend you start doing as soon as you feel comfortable), you'll need to take care of closings. At first this is intimidating, but after you've done one or two it won't bother you at all, especially when you realize how much cash you're saving. Most of the work will be done before the actual closing. You will have arranged financing (if it's not a cash deal), purchased insurance, and provided any documents the other party asked for. When you show up at the closing, read the HUD-1 carefully before you sign it. Make sure you understand each and every charge. If there are any expenses or fees you don't understand, get clarification and negotiate new items if you need to. It will be too late to ask questions after the deal is done, so make sure you resolve any concerns before you sign off on it. Don't be intimidated, ask plenty of questions, and make sure you get answers before you do anything.

174. How long does it take to close?

This will vary from deal to deal, and you want to get each deal done as quickly as you can so you can start cash flowing. My record is six days, but this won't happen very often. Most deals take about thirty days to close. You can help speed up the deal by having all your financials in order, and it's a good idea to review your credit report on a regular basis. It's not unheard of for a closing to be delayed because there was inaccurate information on a credit report that needed to be corrected. You also need to handle any issues that might cloud the title, such as back taxes or probate. Plan ahead and you can avoid the potholes that other people drive into.

175. How do I get the bank to send my mortgage bill to my primary residence and not my rental?

This is a no brainer. The next time you are making a deposit at your bank, stop by your loan officer's desk and tell him that you need the change made. It shouldn't take more than a few minutes to correct. Double check the address you use at the closing and you can avoid this issue.

176. Where can I find the best deals? Will they be foreclosures, short sales, or purchases directly from home owners?

These are all great places to buy property, and you will probably use all three as you build your business. There is no "right" or "wrong" place to buy investment property, except that you have to find the right house at the right time for the right price. Sometimes that will be from a foreclosure, sometimes it will be directly from an owner, and sometimes it will be at a short sale. The key is that you have to go out and find where the best deals are. You can't sit around and wait for the "perfect" house to show up on your doorstep, because that will never happen. Join your local REIA, talk to your friends and family, research online, and talk to your banker, and the deals will start happening.

177. Do I need a home inspection? Who should pay for it?

When you start investing in real estate, you will be tempted to hire an inspector to look at every property. This is especially true if you don't have a background in construction and don't feel comfortable examining foundations or looking at plumbing. I don't do home inspections anymore, mainly because I can't justify the cost on most of the properties I buy. I inspect all the properties myself. You need to start training yourself so that you can be your own inspector. This will save you a ton of cash, and you'll be able to know which properties are going to be moneymakers and which ones will cost you too much to ever cash flow. When you buy right, there is always a margin for error so you don't have to think the world will come to an end if you miss a small problem or two. Talk to your mentor, and ask him how he inspects his properties. If you hire an inspector to look at your first few houses, make sure you go through the house with him and watch what he does. Most reputable inspectors will have a checklist, and they should provide you one when they finish the job. You can use that as a template when you become your own inspector. This may sound intimidating at first, but as you have a few under your belt, your confidence will soar.

178. How do I protect myself from being sued by my tenant?

You can't. The sad reality is that anyone who can afford the filing fees can run down to the courthouse and file a lawsuit even if it has no merit. If you are in business long enough you will eventually be sued, even when you did nothing wrong. What you can do is to prevent as many lawsuits as possible and maximize the chance that you will win when you are sued. The two most important steps are to make sure you follow the law and to document everything. These sound simple, but you'd be amazed at how many people get into trouble just because they didn't have their lease reviewed by an attorney. Most leases are full of "boilerplate" material, and it can be tempting to think you can download any lease from the Internet and use it. Boilerplate leases are fine when things are going well, but if you start having problems, generic clauses you downloaded may not give you the coverage you need. And be sure to create a paper trail so you can prove to the judge what the tenant did or failed to do. If you can't document what you did, it's like it never happened. Protect your business by documenting everything you do.

179. How do I choose good tenants?

You are becoming wise, Grasshopper. If you can answer this question you will avoid many of the problems that plague most investors (and will be ready to snatch the pebble from my hand). Having good tenants is crucial to building your empire. To make good choices about the people who rent your properties, you have to know as much about them before you sign the lease. You need to do a thorough background check (which we will discuss in a moment), and you need to meet with them in person several times before you decide if they are the type of people you want to do business with. You will learn more about a person by spending five minutes with them than you will by talking on the phone with them for hours. Make sure you drive by the addresses listed on the application. Is their current home well cared for? Call the numbers listed for their current jobs, and listen carefully to what you are told. Always trust your gut. You'll never regret passing on a potential tenant if you see red flags. A better prospect will always come along. You can get great leads from your friends, family, current tenants, and the people who own houses next to your rental properties.

180. How do I do a background check?

Your application should always give you permission to run a credit check on your prospects, and that is where you should start. If someone has a history of slow paying creditors (or not paying at all), don't waste any more of your time. Of course, there are reasons where someone might be able to explain a rough patch (such as a divorce or unexpected medical challenges), but if all he has is rough patches, you should pass, especially if he is not able to give any kind of decent explanation as to why he had trouble paying his bills. The next step is to check his criminal record. Most states have this online, and it's fairly easy to run a search of someone's criminal history. Even if it's not online, you can probably drive down to the courthouse and run the search on a computer at the court clerk's office. Again, many people have made mistakes in the past, and a criminal record in and of itself might not be a reason not to rent to someone, especially if it was years ago. But if there are multiple arrests for serious or violent criminal acts and some of them were committed recently, tell Jesse James he needs to look elsewhere for a place to live. Be sure to run every applicant's name through a database of registered sexual offenders. You can bet your neighbors will, and you don't want to have an angry group of them showing up at your office demanding to know why you let a pervert move in next to their kids. If the prospect clears those hurdles, check to see if they have been sued or evicted. Again, people can go through rough times and if the applicant has been evicted or sued that might not mean you're going to have trouble with him, but he needs to be able to explain what happened. And use you common sense. If he has lived in four different places in the last five years and has been evicted from three of them, what are the odds you will have to evict him as well? If you will follow these steps, you can eliminate many of the problems you will have with serial lousy tenants.

181. How long should I lease the property?

We don't lease for longer than a year. If the tenant starts creating problems, we don't want to be locked into a multi-year lease. Plus, this gives us the option of being able to renegotiate the terms every twelve months. We review what other properties in the area are renting for and double-check to make sure we are not under-renting. We also get to do an inspection of the property to make sure there are no problems and that the tenant has maintained it. Once the year is up, if we want to keep the tenant, we have him sign an addendum to the lease and he's good to go for another year.

182. What is a lease?

A lease is a magical piece of paper that is going to make you wealthy and give you a lifestyle most people only dream of. It's the agreement between the property owner and the renter or tenant. It contains all the terms of the agreement, and it's the standard you will use to see if your tenant is in breach of your agreement. When you consistently collect enough of these, you will build your empire and cruise on over to the fast lane.

183. What should be in my lease?

Your lease needs to contain all the important terms of your agreement. It should identify the renter, state the date of the agreement, describe the property, state how much the rent is and when it is due, and define any responsibilities the renter has (such as mowing the yard). Some cities and states require specific language to be included in every lease, so you'll need to understand those requirements and include those. If you ever have a dispute with a tenant and have to take him to court, the judge will look at the lease to decide the case.

184. Should I have an attorney write my lease for me?

You don't have to have an attorney draft your lease (there are many decent ones you can download), but it would probably be worth your time and money to have your lease reviewed. This is especially true when you do your first rental. Having an enforceable lease is extremely important, and this is not an area where you want to be cheap. Paying an attorney for an hour of her time will be much cheaper than having to eat months of rent that you can't collect because your lease wasn't enforceable. Consider having your lease reviewed every few years. Laws change and you don't want to be caught off guard.

185. How do I evict someone?

Sooner or later, you will have a tenant you can't wait to get rid of. Every time you see him you will clench your jaw and wonder why you decided to let him live in your property. Unfortunately, you can't evict someone just because you want to. You have to wait for him to breach the lease. And then, you will have to follow the eviction laws in your state. The eviction process is tightly controlled. You have to do certain things within a certain time, and if you miss a day or if your paperwork isn't exactly as it is supposed to be, you may have to start over and that means delaying your cash flow. Generally, you start by sending the tenant a "Notice to Quit," which is a letter outlining how he has breached the lease and how he can correct the problem. If he owes back rent, for example, he will have a certain number of days to pay it (usually five) and if he doesn't you can file a civil suit asking a judge to give you the right to evict him. Once the suit is filed, you have to give him notice of it a certain number of days before the hearing. You can't show up on his doorstep at midnight the night before the hearing and try to surprise him with the paperwork. And many places require you to hire a process server (who has to be on an approved list) to deliver the paperwork. After you have given proper notice, there is a hearing before the judge. It will be your job to prove the tenant has breached the agreement, and that is why it is so important that you document everything that has happened. The judge will listen to you, and then he will listen to the tenant. This may come as a shock to most of you, but some people will lie through their teeth, even when they have been placed under oath. If you've done your homework and prepared properly, you can explain to the judge how your tenant is full of crap, and the judge will rule in your favor. But wait, it's not over yet. Now you actually have to get the tenant to vacate the property. Once the judge enters his order, the tenant will have a certain number of days to get out. Hopefully, he'll pack up his stuff and move on, but if he doesn't, you'll have to have the sheriff come out and remove him. I know this sounds really complicated, and I'm not trying to intimidate you. But I do want you to understand how important it is for you to document when your tenant breaches the lease. It's also important for you to understand the eviction process in your area so that you can lawfully get rid of deadbeat tenants and replace them with people who are going to put money in your pockets.

186. Should I pay a company to manage my rental properties?

Hiring a management company can be a great way to build your empire. They can take care of finding new tenants, collecting rent, and taking care of any maintenance and repairs. You sit back and wait for the check to roll in each month. Of course, management companies charge for their services, so you will need to factor that into your deals. Management fees range from 8 to 12 percent, and 10 percent is a common practice. When you only own a few local properties, hiring a management company may not make sense. But as your empire grows (or if you buy out of town properties), hiring the right company is the only way to go. I plan on hiring someone to take care of all of my properties. This is going to free me up to put together deals, instead of worrying about leaky toilets.

187. What's the best way to collect rent?

There are only three ways you should collect the rent: the tenants should mail you a check, hand deliver a check to your office, or arrange for the amount to be debited out of their bank accounts. Period. You should never, ever, physically go to their house to collect rent. That is not your job. You are trying to build a multi-million dollar company, and you have to start acting like one. Does your bank send someone out to get a mortgage check from you each month? Does the financial institution that financed your car come track you down each month? Or do these companies expect you to be responsible enough to get your checks to them on time? Don't waste your time tracking down tenants each month. It's their responsibility to get the payment to you.

188. What are renter's rights?

These are the minimum rights tenants are granted under the law. They will vary from state to state, so you'll have to verify this with your attorney, but here are a few of the ones you will find in almost every state: tenants have the right to be free from discrimination; they have the right for the property to be habitable (it has to be structurally sound, have adequate utilities, and meet all health and safety codes); they have the right to access the property; they have the right for the utilities to work (assuming they have paid the bill) and the landlord cannot stop the utilities from working; they have the right for any necessary repairs to be made in a timely manner; and their personal property cannot be encumbered or interfered with unless the landlord has a court order. Make sure you understand what renter's rights are in your area or it may end up costing you big time.

189. Should I allow pets?

Fido may be a tenant's best friend, but he can be a landlord's worst enemy. Pets will pee on carpets, scratch paint, and make houses stink. You will need to thoroughly clean your property after a pet owner moves out, and you should factor that into your deposits. We allow small pets, and we charge a $250 non-refundable deposit. We don't allow any pets over forty pounds. Larger dogs cause more damage to property, and no amount of money is worth having to clean up after them.

190. I just lost my house, and I want to move in to my rental. How do I get my tenant to leave?

If he is under a lease and hasn't breached it, you can't force him out. You would have to wait until the lease expires and then not renew it. However, you could offer him an incentive (such as cash) to leave early. But unless he breaches the lease or agrees to move out, you will have to find another place to live. Of course, some investors include a thirty day notice provision in their leases, which allows the parties to cancel the agreement with thirty days written notice. Visit with your attorney to see if this is enforceable in your area or if this is something you want to include in your lease.

191. Can I raise the rent on my tenant? When and how much?

In general, you can raise the rent anytime a lease is up, and you can charge whatever you want. The exception is if your property is in a "rent controlled" area. These areas have strong restrictions on when the rent can be raised and how much the increase can be. Be wary about buying property in rent controlled areas, because these restrictions prevent you from doing what you want with your investment. Keep in mind, however, even if you are able to raise the rent whenever you want, you need to make sure the rent is in line with other properties in the area. If you rent is too high, tenants will vote with their feet and move somewhere else.

192. I recently started investing in real estate with two partners. I put in 1/3 of the investment and should get 1/3 of the profit. How can I make sure they are honest with me regarding expenses for repairing the property and the selling price?

If you have any questions about their honesty, you should never have gone into business with them. The basis of any relationship is trust, and this is especially true when money is involved. Never enter into any partnership without a written agreement. It should outline who pays what, how profits are going to be divided, how expenses are going to be accounted for, and who has a say over the sale of the property. If you don't have a written partnership agreement at the beginning of your venture, you are virtually doomed to fail.

193. Is it better to invest in residential or commercial real estate?

Neither one of these is "better" than the other. Some people do great things with residential, others do commercial, and some do both. There are advantages and disadvantages to both, and you have to find what works for you and gives you the most opportunities. In The Savvy Landlord, I had the opportunity to interview several successful real estate investors, and I asked every one of them whether they preferred residential or commercial. Every one of them had a strong opinion, but the consensus was that people should build their empires with single-family units. I agree, but you have to find what works for you. Make some deals, see what you like and what works for you, learn from your mistakes and successes, and then do some more deals. You will find your niche. One theme that many investors have expressed to me is that commercial buildings can be vacant for quite a while. It's not unusual for an office building or warehouse to be without a tenant for months (or in some case, years). Be prepared for that if you decide to invest in commercial buildings.

194. What are the fastest and best ways to find commercial property/deals?

The only way to find deals is to work your butt off. Join your local REIA, start networking, get in your car and drive around commercial areas to find properties that are for sale, and scour the classified ads in the newspaper. Loopnet.com is a great website, and you can call every commercial Realtor you can find. You won't do any deals by sitting on the couch thinking about how great it's going to be once you find some properties. Quit dreaming about getting deals done, and go do some deals.

195. How do I prepare to start investing in real estate properties?

It's important to educate yourself. Read as much as you can. Join your local REIA and ask as many questions as you can think of. Attend a real estate auction or two to see how they are done. Also, make sure your financial information is in order. You'll have to borrow money to build your empire, so make sure you have your tax returns and banking information ready for your banker to review. Pull a copy of your credit report and make sure there are no mistakes or issues that need to be resolved. Find a mentor you trust and who is willing to work with you. And then go out and do some deals.

196. Is buying properties in other states a good idea?

Buying the right properties in other states can be a great way to build your empire. But the numbers have to work, and the properties have to fit in your portfolio. Don't buy out of state property just to say you own property out of state. If the purchase is a good business decision, there is no reason not to do it. But there are two factors you should take into consideration. First, landlord-tenant laws in the other state may be different than they are in your home state, and you need to understand them before you invest. Second, you need to decide how you will maintain and repair the property. Hiring a management company can be a great way to do this. But you have to factor that cost into the deal when you crunch the numbers.

197. What type of research do I need to do before a make a purchase?

The short version is that you have to make sure the property makes more money than it costs you. This means you have to know what the property costs, how much the property taxes and insurance will be, how much it will cost to repair or rehab it, and how long it will take for the property to be rent-ready. You also have to know how much you can rent the property for, and this means understanding your market. If you see a "For Rent" sign on a house near a property you are interested in buying, call the owner and find out what the rent is. But the best way to know what is a fair rent is to become experienced in the neighborhoods where you want to own houses. Once you have done a few deals, you'll be able to walk a property and have a pretty good idea if it will cash flow or not.

198. Are there any books you would recommend?

You can't read too much about real estate when you decide to become an investor. There's a lot of great information out there, and all you have to do is make the effort to educate yourself. I'm proud of my book, The Savvy

Landlord, and I've received a lot of positive feedback. Hopefully, that will be a great starting place. Of course, I highly recommend Rich Dad, Poor Dad. That book changed my life and the lives of millions of other investors. But you have to find the books that work for you. You can order a ton of them online, or you can read them for free by checking them out from your local library. Your education is in your hands, and there is no excuse for you not to seek out as many books as you can handle.

199. Where would be the best place to invest right now?

There are no magic places. You have to invest in the properties that fit in your portfolio and goals, and that will help you make the most money as quickly as possible. Most newbies buy their first few properties in the city where they live. It's comforting to be able to visit the property when they need to. But you may find properties in another city (or even another state) that you can use to build your empire, and you should take advantage of these opportunities when you have the chance. But you have to do your due diligence. You may think that buying in a place like California or Florida can be great, but you have to do enough research to make sure you'll cash flow on the deal. Don't get caught up in owning property in a particular area code. Be savvy by buying the right property at the right time, regardless of where it is.

200. Should real estate taxes play a part in purchasing a property?

You should always factor real estate taxes into your deals. It's part of your due diligence, and if you don't factor these costs in when you crunch your numbers you will lose money. Never pull the trigger on a property without knowing how much the real estate taxes will be. Taxes eat profit and cash flow, and assume the property taxes will increase over the next few years.

When taxes go up, cash flow goes down, and you need to be prepared for that.

201. What kind of special insurance do I need on my investment properties?

It is important for you to talk about your insurance needs with an agent who is familiar and experienced with real estate investors. The stakes are high, and a good agent can make sure you have enough protection to take care of you in the event something goes wrong. At a minimum, you need liability insurance (which will protect you in the event someone is hurt on your property) and general property insurance (which will protect your property in the event it is damaged by things such as fire, flood, or tornados). You'll need to have policy limits that are high enough to cover any judgment against you or to repair the property so it can quickly be rent-ready. I've heard of some investors who don't have insurance, and this makes no sense to me. I've worked hard to build my business, and I have no intention of losing everything after a bad storm rolls through.

202. Where can I get insurance for investment properties?

You need to find an agent who has worked with investors in the past. Insuring investment properties is not the same as writing a policy for car or residential properties. Plus, an experienced agent can help you avoid problems. You can find the right agent by asking your mentor or some of the experienced investors you meet at your REIA. But don't expect to find the right person by pulling out a name from the phone book. It's going to take time and effort on your part, but the rewards are worth it. A few companies that insure investment properties are Shelter, Allstate, and American Modern.

203. Are there any additional expenses incurred when buying investment properties?

There are always expenses when you own real estate property. You will have to repair and maintain your properties, and sometimes it seems like you are constantly fixing toilets or painting walls. It is just a part of the business and you have to understand that going in. You have to factor in these costs when you do your deals so that you cash flow as much as possible. Don't expect to buy properties and then forget about them. Investing in rentals is a great way to build financial freedom, but you have to spend time and money maintaining your properties.

204. How does rental property management software work? Can you recommend one?

Rental property software is a great way to track your expenses and income on each property. With a few clicks of your mouse you can see how much money you are making. You can also generate invoices, track vendors and work orders, and collect rent. If you're not using property management software, you're putting your foot on the brake when it should be on the gas pedal. There are several excellent programs, and if you do an online search you can find one that meets your needs. We use buildium.com and highly recommend it.

205. How can I find a real estate investment mentor?

The best way is to join your local REIA. If you attend these meetings regularly, you will meet a lot of great people who are willing to help you grow your empire. You'll probably click with one or two of them, and then you can visit with them about mentoring you. Make sure you connect with the right person. You don't want to get tangled up with some wannabe who looks the part but hasn't done any real deals. Ask if you can join him when he inspects a property or does a closing. A great mentor will put you on the fast track to success. The wrong one will drag you down and prevent you from reaching your goals.

206. Is it possible for an amateur to be successful in real estate investing?

Have we met? When I started investing, I didn't know anything about owning or managing property. I was as amateur and uneducated as I could be. And I still managed to build a multi-million dollar portfolio. If I can do it, anyone can. If you work hard, educate yourself, and learn from each deal, you won't be a newbie for long. And that's when things start getting fun and the cash starts rolling in.

207. I am a first-time home buyer and investor. Should I buy a duplex?

Buying a duplex can be a great way for newbies to get in the game, especially if they plan on living in one unit of the property while the tenant makes the mortgage payment. But living next to a tenant can be very frustrating, especially if you have the wrong tenant or if the property needs work. You don't want a tenant to show up at your door every time the toilet keeps running or if a faucet starts dripping. Keep that in mind if you plan on living in one of the units. You also have to address issues involving common areas. For example, who is responsible for mowing the grass? If you take care of these things when you sign your lease, owning a duplex can be a great way to start your empire.

208. Can I ask the seller of an investment property to reduce the price for an all cash deal?

Absolutely. Savvy investors negotiate on almost everything, and this includes the sales price of property and asking for a discount for cash payment. If a buyer is willing to pay cash, it means the seller won't have to jump through all the hoops of dealing with a bank. This makes the process quicker and easier, and it eliminates the uncertainty of financing a property. There is a lot of value to the seller in accepting cash, so don't be afraid to ask for a discount. The worst thing that will happen is that the seller says no.

209. Is sales tax charged for buying an investment property?

No. Trust me, you'll have plenty of opportunities to pay sales tax, but you won't have to pay it when you buy properties. At least not yet. Maybe I should change the subject before I give anybody any ideas.

210. What are my rights when I buy an investment property? Are they the same as when I buy residential property?

Yes. When you buy investment property you are free to do with as you please, just like when you buy a residence. However, you may have fewer rights when you lease the property to a tenant. The landlord-tenant laws that apply will restrict you to your area. You won't be able to make certain changes to the property if you have rented it out. You will also be bound by the terms of the lease. It sounds odd, but even though you own the property your rights will be restricted when you sign a lease.

211. How do I find out how much is still owed on a property?

This can be a little tricky. In most places, there won't be a database telling you the balance on a mortgage. But you can learn a lot by looking at the records at the county courthouse. If you get lucky, there will be a release filed, which means the property is owned free and clear. If not, you should still be able to see when the mortgage was created. You should be able to see the amount originally due and be able to calculate the balance based on the number of years left. If all else fails, ask the owner or the bank. Some of them will be reluctant to tell you, but if you catch them in the right mood and they're ready to sell, you may get a straight answer.

212. Is selling an investment property different than selling a residential property?

Yes, there is a world of difference. When you sell investment property, the buyer is looking at the deal to see if he can make money. If you put a lot of money into expensive upgrades, fancy carpet, or top of the line appliances, you'll have to raise your selling price. This may make the deal too skinny for investors, and you may have a hard time getting the money you need. When you sell a residential property, you have to make sure every detail is perfect. You want to have the best of everything, and your buyers aren't looking at the property as a money making investment. They are buying a home. It's where they will celebrate holidays and where their children will sleep, and you have to sell them that dream. I tried to flip a property a few years ago, and I learned the hard way that you can't treat rental properties the same way you treat residential properties. Don't make the same mistake I did.

213. What is a fixture?

When some investors hear the word "fixture," they think about light fixtures. In real estate terms, fixture means anything that is permanently attached to the property that cannot be removed without damage to the structure. Ceiling fans, stoves, dishwashers, and sinks are fixtures. Fixtures are usually included as part of the property, so if there are any fixtures in a property you want to keep (such as antique ceiling fans), you need to remove them before you show the house or make sure the sales contract clearly states which fixtures are included and which ones are not. It's a small detail but you don't want to buy a property assuming the stove and dishwasher were included, only to find out at the closing that you will have to buy new ones.

214. How do I increase the value of my investment property?

You start increasing the value of your property the day you buy it. Most real estate will appreciate naturally over time, and you can maximize this by not overpaying for property and buying in the right locations. If you pay too much or put your money in the wrong neighborhood, the price will almost never increase to the point that you get value out of it. You also have to take care of the basic maintenance. When one of your properties needs to be painted, if the carpet or flooring is worn out, if termites are eating the foundation, or if the toilets are leaking, fix it as soon as you can. These things will not get better by themselves, and you can't wish these issues away. If you don't take care of them when they are small, they will only grow and your empire will crumble around you. You can also increase the value of your property by making some basic improvements. When a stove is outdated, replace it with a new one. When the water heater goes out, do some research and replace it with the best one that fits in your budget.

Upgrade the landscaping. Before you do anything, of course, you need to run the numbers and make sure it fits within your budget. By keeping on top of the basic maintenance and making a few, inexpensive upgrades, you can help your properties reach their maximum values.

215. I've heard and seen the words "1031 exchange." What does that mean?

Section 1031 is a provision of the tax code. It's important to investors because it allows you to buy and sell within certain timeframes and defer any capital gains taxes. You should visit with your accountant about this, but if you sell one property and purchase another one of "like kind" within the timeframes of Section 1031, you qualify for the exchange. You have to identify the properties within a certain number of days, and then make the exchange within another set of days, but if you want to replace one house with another one this can be a great tax strategy.

216. Is the cost of landscaping my properties worth it?

Yes. I used to think the cost wasn't worth it, but I've learned that a property with a manicured, landscaped lawn can be leased for higher rent than one with a plain yard. It's a small investment that will make you a lot of money. Plus, when you decide to sell the property you'll be able to sell it for a higher amount if the yard is well cared for.

217. I've seen some properties where attached garages are converted into bedrooms. Are those worth the investment?

Absolutely. Your job as an investor is to make as much money as possible, and conversions are an easy way to increase the value of your properties.

A conversion will change a three-bedroom property into a four-bedroom, and you can increase your rent accordingly. Conversions are a great way to invest your money and build your empire. Convert garages whenever it fits into your investment strategy and goals.

218. I haven't been able to talk with one of my tenants for two weeks. What should I do?

Does he owe you rent, or do you just miss him? Unless he has breached the lease or you have reason to think something has happened to him don't worry about it. Adults do that from time to time. We take vacations and want time to ourselves. Put that energy into taking care of your family. Your tenant will find his way home. And if he doesn't, start the eviction process.

219. One of my tenants took it upon herself to make a repair. She attached a receipt for the parts to her rent check and wants a deduction. What should I do?

In some cases, tenants are allowed to make necessary repairs and deduct the amount from their rent. But they can only do that in specific circumstances, such as when the repair is needed to make the property safe or habitable. And they have to give you written notice before they undertake the repairs themselves. If you don't repair the property within a certain number of days, the tenant is allowed to deduct the charges from her next rent payment. But a tenant can't repair something simple like a leaking toilet and then try to pass the charges on to you. When a tenant mentions your property needs repairs (especially if it involves leaking water or problems with a major system like the foundation or electricity), have your handyman look at it as quickly as possible. It's the right thing to do, and those kinds of problems can damage your investment and take money out of your pocket. Plus, if you deal with those problems as soon as you hear about them, your tenant won't have anything to complain about and you will avoid any issues about discounts to the rent. Of course, if the repair is minor and the tenant asks in advance, we're willing to let her spend the money and then deduct it from the rent. But we don't make a habit of this.

220. A tenant skipped out in the middle of the night. What do I do?

If this hasn't happened to you yet, prepare yourself. Because sooner or later one of your tenants will pull a midnight move and leave you high and dry. The first thing you need to do is to inspect the property. Look for any damage and calculate how much it's going to cost to get the property rent-ready. Be sure to document any expenses so you can recover them from the tenant when you take him to court. And then start the eviction process. This can be frustrating when you know the tenant has moved and you need the cash flow from renting the property. But you still have to jump through all the legal hurdles so you can collect any back rent or damages the deadbeat owes you. Once you have a court order, you can go into the property and find someone better to take his place.

221. Who pays for the light bulbs?

The general rule is that the landlord would be responsible for paying for bulbs in public areas, such as the stairwells in apartment complexes or condos. But tenants pay for bulbs in private areas, such as bedrooms and kitchens. When you get a property ready to show to prospects, one of the items on your checklist should be to make sure all the bulbs are working. It's a small detail, but you want everything to look as professional as you can, and some people will take a burned out light bulb as a lack of professionalism on your part. Don't give them any reason to rent from someone else, or to call you with petty concerns like a light bulb. Plus, some people will call the maintenance man when a bulb is burned out, and this will cost you money.

222. Should I invest in condos?

I have talked to hundreds of other investors, and condos are rarely mentioned as a great way to build wealth in real estate investing. I suppose there could be a great opportunity in condos, but most investors stick to single-family units, other multi-unit properties (such as apartments or duplexes), or commercial properties. A few of the problems with condos include HOA (home owners' association) fees, issues involving common areas such as the roof, and neighbors who don't maintain their property. It's better to stick with single-family units or with multi-family units where you can buy the entire property.

223. Do I have to pay HOA Fees?

If the property is subject to any covenants that require HOA fees, you will need to pay them. HOA fees pay for the upkeep of certain common areas, such as swimming pools, and if they aren't paid, the association can take the property owner to court. There have been a few court cases in recent years where associations have been very aggressive and have been awarded judgments against owners. In a few cases, the properties were auctioned off to satisfy the balance due on the fees. Of course, you can make it a term of the lease that the tenant pays any HOA fees. When you are doing your due diligence, make sure you understand if the property is subject to HOA assessments, how much they are, and when they are due. If the tenant agrees to pay them, be sure to follow up and verify they pay them on time.

224. Should I put window units or Central Heat & Air in a rental?

We install window units in our properties when it makes sense. We can't justify the cost of putting in central systems unless we see a return. Sometimes, it takes too long to recoup the investment. In this business it's all about the cash flow, and every penny matters. Your job as an investor is to provide safe, habitable housing at a competitive price. You don't have to install every conceivable option. As long as the window units cool and heat the property, you've done your job. Of course, every property is different, and we take as many factors as possible (including the location) into consideration when deciding which type of air conditioning to install.

225. How do I garnish a tenant's wages after I have been awarded a judgment against him?

Once you have a judgment against a tenant, turn it over to a collection agency or an attorney who specializes in debt collection. Debt collection is controlled by a lot of state and federal laws (such as the Fair Debt Collection Act), and if don't follow the exact procedure you may not be able to collect the debt. In the worst case scenario, you could even end up owing the tenant money. Leave it to the professionals and let them use their resources to get your money. Your time is too valuable to spend it trying to make a deadbeat pay a few hundred dollars. Spend your time looking for deals that are going to make you thousands or tens of thousands of dollars.

226. How do move-in specials work as incentives to attract tenants?

Marketing is an important part of your business, just like it is with any other company. Move-in specials can be a great way to bring new, qualified tenants into your properties. A lot of landlords will offer a free month to new tenants who sign a year-long lease. If you look at the numbers, that comes out to be an 8 percent discount over a twelve-month lease. It's worth a few hundred dollars to get dependable tenants in your units. You might also think about giving away televisions, game systems, or even a computer or tablet. You would be amazed at what you can buy for about a month's rent, and that can be the difference between a prospect renting from you or your competition.

227. My tenant doesn't want to renew his lease and wants to go month-to-month. What should I do?

I'm assuming he's been a good tenant and you want to keep him around. If he is, you want to do everything you can to keep him as long as possible. If not, this is your chance to get rid of him. Before his lease expires, notify him that if he does not renew his lease and that he will be on a month-to-month tenancy. There should also be a reasonable increase in his rent. A signed lease gives you a certain amount of security, and you should only give that up if the new monthly rent makes it worth your while. Of course, at some point you will have to decide when it is no longer worth your time to have him on a month to month and rent the property to a tenant on a regular lease. Here is how we handle it. If he is intent on being on a month to month, we increase the rent by $50 a month. If he signs a six-month lease, the increase is only $25, and if he signs a year-long lease, the rent stays the same. Hopefully, the savings is enough to motivate the tenant to stay.

228. What is a double-closing?

After you've been in the business a while, you'll probably buy property as part of a double-closing. To put it simply (and as its name implies), two closings happen at once. It typically involves a seller, a flipper or wholesaler, and a buyer. Here's how it works. The seller and wholesaler have a property under contract, and they close on that deal. Then the wholesaler immediately sells it to the buyer. It's a great deal for everyone. The seller makes money from the sale to the wholesaler, the wholesaler makes money on the sale to the buyer, and the buyer has another piece of property in his portfolio.

229. What does "subject to" mean?

"Subject to" means you are buying a property with an existing mortgage, but instead of paying with cash or using your own financing to do the deal, you are taking over the seller's payments. It's being purchased "subject to" the existing mortgage. This can be a great way to add properties to your empire. Make sure the seller puts the deed in a trust. If not and he files bankruptcy, you could lose the property.

230. What is an assignable contract?

An assignable contract is one that allows the buyer to transfer his rights in the property to a third party. This is a very common practice with wholesalers. In fact, it is how they make their money. They get a property under contract and then sell or assign their rights to a buyer for a profit. Some sales contracts don't allow the rights of the buyer to be assigned, so if you're interested in wholesaling be sure to read the fine print. If you want to create the right to assign a contract, make sure that instead of just signing your name as owner of your company you include the phrase, "and assigns." For example, you would sign the sales contract as, "John Smith and assigns." This gives you the right to assign your interest in the contract to anyone you see fit.

231. I saw a "For Sale" sign that read, "Owner/Agent." What does that mean?

This means that the owner is real estate agent. Real estate agents are heavily regulated, and they are required to disclose when they own a piece of property they are selling. It's okay to buy one of these properties, but make sure you do your research. Most Realtors will be seasoned, and if you don't do your homework you may get taken for a ride and pay more than you have to.

232. Should I buy at an auction?

I will always have a soft spot for auctions. After all, I bought my first properties at auctions. You can find some great deals at auctions, but you have to make sure the properties meet your goals, and you have to keep your emotions in check. Once the bidding starts, it can be easy to get caught up in the moment. Things can get very competitive, and it's easy to find yourself in a bidding war. Make things easier by attending an auction or two before you are ready to start bidding. If you have an idea of how things go, you won't be distracted by the unfamiliar. And have a set spending limit. After you make a few bids on a property, you might feel emotionally invested and if you stick to a preset limit you won't wake up with any regrets the next day.

233. How many houses do I need to look at to find a deal?

Real estate investing is a numbers game. You will have to look at a lot of houses before you find one that fits into your portfolio, but there is no set number. But some investors say you have to look at 100 properties before you find a good deal. Don't get discouraged. Sometimes, you will find several houses back to back that you want to buy, but soon after you may go weeks or months before you find a decent house at the right price. Keep moving forward and look at as many properties as you can. You will find the right properties.

234. How many offers do I need to submit to get deal? Is there a formula or ratio?

Again, real estate investing is a numbers game. Make as many serious offers as you can, and things will fall into place. A savvy investor once told me I would have to submit an average of ten offers to close one deal. If you haven't been able to buy properties after making several offers, you may need to tweak your strategy. Are your offers reasonable? Were they packaged professionally? If you are making mistakes, learn from them so you can close the next deal you bid on.

235. My Realtor is asking me to write a blank check so he can submit offers. Should I do that?

I'm sorry. I didn't hear your question. I was too busy imagining your Realtor sipping daiquiris on a beach in a country with no extradition treaty while you were crying at home wondering what happened to all of your money. Never, ever, give anyone a blank check. There is no valid business reason for this, and no good will ever come from it. If you are ever in a situation where you have to prove your ability to pay for a property, use an escrow account. No one will be able to transfer funds out of it without your permission, and it will eliminate the temptation that someone would face when she looks at the blank check you just gave her. That being said, here is one technique I use to speed things along. I have known my Realtor for years and have total trust in him. I sent him a copy of a blank check. If he needs to, he can fill in the numbers and attach it to an offer. However, it's not like he can run down to the bank and cash it. And I wouldn't do that if I didn't know him so well or had any questions about his character or honesty.

236. A Realtor tried to get me to sign an exclusive investor buying agreement at closing. I didn't sign it, but I wonder if that is common practice.

No, this is not common, and you did the right thing by not signing it. What the Realtor was trying to do was to limit your options as far as where you can buy property. She wanted you to agree that you wouldn't buy any properties unless you did them through her, even if you found the property on your own. It's okay to work with Realtors (in fact, if you're not, you are costing yourself money), but you don't want to limit your options. Don't sign anything that would prevent you from finding your own deals or that would keep other people from referring potential properties to you.

237. Not only did the Realtor/broker representing me make a commission from an investment property I purchased, he charged me a $250 transaction fee. Is that a normal business practice?

I'm not sure I would call it "normal," but some Realtors and brokers will charge a transaction fee in addition to their commissions. However, they have to disclose this to you up front. If it's never been discussed and the charge suddenly appears at the closing, I wouldn't pay it. And I might refuse to do business with the Realtor/broker again. It's one thing to agree to pay fees for services rendered, but it's another to be strong-armed into paying more than you have to. Be sure to review all costs at every closing and don't sign anything until every question you have has been answered. Once the paperwork is signed, the deal is done and you'll be on the hook.

238. I saw a foreclosure sign on a property. Can I contact the bank directly?

It depends. Some banks make you go through a Realtor, but nothing is stopping you from calling them directly to see if you can do a deal. In fact, some banks will have their contact information on the sign to encourage you to call them. Anytime you see a property that looks like it would fit into your portfolio, be proactive and start calling the seller. Most deals aren't going to find you. You will have to go out and find them. You can't sit in your office waiting for the phone to ring or for people to walk through the door with great contracts for you to sign. Get out and make things happen, and that includes calling lenders about their foreclosures. They will let you know if you need to get a Realtor involved, and then he can make the call for you.

239. What is a "lowball" offer?

A "lowball" offer is when a buyer makes a ridiculously low offer on a property. You should always be shrewd when negotiating, but you have to be careful about lowballing people. It may work once in a while with a newbie or with someone who is desperate to unload a property, but if you do it with seasoned investors you won't be taken seriously. Savvy investors know the value of their properties, and they won't waste their time dealing with people who either don't understand the market or are trying to buy properties for pennies on the dollar. Not only will lowballing cost you the deal you made the offer on, the seller may remember your offer, take it as an insult, and refuse to do any future business with you. Lowballing may make you a few dollars in the short term, but it may cost you thousands in the long run. Be a tough negotiator, but don't waste anybody's time by making absurdly low offers.

240. I was trying to do my annual inspection of a rental property, but the tenant would not let me see it. What should I do?

Take out a copy of the deed and look at the name of the owner. It lists your name, right? You own the property, and you have the right to inspect it. Document the tenant's refusal, send him a letter setting a specific time when you will make your inspection (make sure you give him at least twenty-four hours), and inspect your property. Include a copy of the lease he signed and highlight the clause that gives you permission to make an inspection. If you show up and he has changed the locks or has physically blocked your access, don't force your way in. Start the eviction process, get an order forcing him out, document the condition of the property, and bill him for every penny it cost to repair the property. It's your property and no one has the right to keep you from making an inspection.

241. My tenant just informed me the next door neighbor built a fence on the property. What should I do?

The first thing you need to do is inspect the property and make sure the fence is actually on your property. Don't assume the tenant is correct or rely on his word without documenting the facts. You don't want to alienate your neighbor if he hasn't done anything wrong. If you aren't clear as to where the property line is, send a polite letter to the neighbor stating you are concerned about the fence encroaching on your property. This may sound weak to some people, but it is always better to avoid a fight than it is to win one. Suppose you send a threatening letter to the neighbor, and then it turns out the fence isn't on your property? You just burned that bridge, and this may cost you money in the future when he refuses to call you when he hears water gushing from a broken pipe or when he sees someone breaking into the property but "doesn't want to get involved."

Plus, if the issue ever goes to court, he will wave that letter in front of the judge, and it won't help your case. Make sure your letter has a firm but polite tone, and it won't bite you in the rear later on. If the neighbor doesn't respond to the letter, if he doesn't care or tells you to kiss off, hire a lawyer or a surveyor. You don't want to rush down to the courthouse without doing your due diligence, because if you're wrong and the fence is not on your property you may end up paying for costs and your neighbor's attorney fees. Take it slow, get as much information as possible, and don't pick a fight if you don't have to.

242. A tree on one of my properties fell onto the next door neighbor's car and smashed the window and hood. Do I pay for that?

No. It is their property and that is why they pay for insurance. I had this happen once, and my agent and adjuster refused to pay. But this is a perfect example of why you need liability insurance for each of your properties. When you are have been investing for a while, you are bound to have things go wrong, and this includes having tree branches crush someone else's property. When you get a call from the neighbor, give him you insurance agent's telephone number, and then call your agent and let him know what happened. Let them handle the issue so that you don't have to deal with a neighbor who is angry about his damaged car.

243. What is an ARM loan?

ARM stands for "adjustable rate mortgage." It is a mortgage that gives the lender the right to adjust the interest rate depending on changes to a specified index. The changes can only be made at intervals specified in the mortgage. I'm not a big fan of ARMs, because I want my costs to be fixed and reliable. Some investors have gotten into trouble the last few years when their mortgages increased so much they had trouble making the payments. If you use ARMs, be careful and plan for the worst.

244. How do I reduce my closing costs?

I hate closing costs. They are too expensive, and if I could find a way to eliminate them, I would do it in a heartbeat. And it's not just me. I've spoken to dozens of other investors and we all feel the same. But banks and title companies are going to make their money, and that means buyers are going to foot the bill. Closing costs are part of doing business. The best way to reduce your closing costs is to review each and every sales contract with a fine-toothed comb. Don't pay for anything you don't understand or that you didn't agree to, and remember that everything is negotiable until you sign the paperwork. Ask for a discount on the costs, and remind them you are an investor and will be closing on many other properties in the future. Hopefully, the thought of repeat business will be enough of an incentive to lower the fees. Be savvy, but not greedy, and negotiate everything you can. You might also consider having a lawyer do the closing, as opposed to using a title company. An experienced attorney can probably get the job done for a cheaper price.

245. What's the best way to close? Should we do it at a title company or at a lawyer's office?

Most closings are done at the title company. They are pretty thorough, and there probably won't be any issues at the closing. But if there are, you will have access to the people who prepared the abstract, made the decision to underwrite the insurance, and cleared the title. That's a lot easier than trying to reach them by phone if you have any questions during the closing. Of course, when you buy title insurance you won't have to worry about this.

246. What is title insurance?

Title insurance is a policy that protects buyers from any problem in the title, such as any liens or problems with the chain of ownership. I won't buy property without it. It's dirt cheap (usually only a few hundred dollars per property), which is much cheaper than it would cost to hire a lawyer for a quiet title action. I've never had to use it, but it doesn't make any sense to take the risk and not purchase it.

247. My tenant is claiming that there are repairs that need to be fixed and is not paying the rent until I fix them. What are my options?

A tenant cannot refuse to pay the rent because repairs need to be made. In some cases, they can notify you in writing of problems that make the property uninhabitable or unsanitary and you have to make the repairs in a certain number of days. But you have to be given the chance to make the repairs before he can withhold rent. If you get a letter from a tenant stating something major needs to be fixed, take care of it as quickly as you can. You're not necessarily doing it for the tenant. You're doing it to preserve your investment. Thinking that way makes it easier to pay for a new roof or sewer pipe. And be sure to document the situation with a letter explaining the law and the fact the tenant needs to pay the rent.

248. Is it a good idea to have a Realtor lease my properties for me while I manage them?

Yes, in fact, I do this all the time. The Realtor finds the tenants, and I pay her a fee when the lease is signed. This frees up a lot of my time and makes things simpler so I can put deals together. That's where the real money is. Pay someone to lease the properties, cash the rent checks, and pull the trigger on your next purchase.

249. How do I stop my tenant from parking on the grass?

Where do people get the idea it's okay to treat the front yard like a parking slab? I mean seriously, who taught them it they could park on the grass? I know I didn't, and I'm sure my neighbors who worked hard to buy their houses didn't sign off on it. In case you couldn't tell, this is a big issue for me. I can't stand it when a tenant drives his car up to the front door and then leaves it in the yard. I didn't work so hard to build my portfolio so that a few rednecks could make it look like a scene from "The Beverly Hillbillies." So once I see a car parked in the yard, I do everything I can to get Jethro to learn to use the driveway. The first thing I do is to call code enforcement. Parking on the lawn is illegal, and every time I see it happening at one of my properties I call and report a code violation in the neighborhood to protect my investments. That's usually all it takes. But if the tenant doesn't get the message, I start having my friends and family call, too. The complaints are anonymous, so I don't have to worry that the tenant will know I'm the one who reported him. If the tenant still doesn't get the hint, I refuse to rent to him when the lease is up. It may seem like a petty issue, but parking on the grass is just the tip of the iceberg. If you don't nip that in the bud, it won't be long before you start seeing other problems, like dogs running loose and trash in the yard. And this spreads like a disease, and soon your neighbors will stop taking care of their properties, too. Always maintain an attitude of professionalism, and expect your tenants to do the same.

250. Can I hire a collection agency to collect back rent on a dead-beat tenant?

Yes. Not only can you do it, you should always do it. Never waste your time by personally trying to collect money from deadbeats. The same time and energy you spend prying a few hundred dollars out of some loser who doesn't want to pay you could be spent finding deals that are going to put tens of thousands of dollars in your pockets. I'm not saying you should let the guy off the hook, but hire a collection firm to make the calls and collect the money. They can also handle all the liability. Focus your energy on making real money and creating a lifestyle most people only dream of.

251. How much deprecation can I claim on my rental property?

As much as Uncle Sam lets you. Rental property is usually depreciated over a 27.5 year period, but this is an area you should confirm with your accountant. And you will only be able to depreciate the value of the house, not the land (land never loses its value). For example, assume you buy a property for $75,000. If the county assessor values the house at $50,000 and the land at $25,000, you could depreciate the $50,000 at $1,818 per year ($50,000 divided by 27.5).

252. I just purchased a rental house and received a notice that the property taxes are increasing. How do I reduce the taxes?

You will have to file an appeal with the assessment board. Property taxes are based on a percentage of the assessed value of your home. One of two things has happened to increase your taxes. Either the percentage everyone is required to pay has gone up or your home has been assessed at a higher value. If the percentage has increased, it's made the taxes for every property go up and you won't have much luck fighting this. But if the increase is due to an increase on the assessment, you can file an appeal and argue that the appeal is either inaccurate or a mistake. Due to the downturn in the real estate market, many homeowners have seen their home values plummet, and many of them have been able to appeal their assessments and reduce their taxes. If your property taxes unexpectedly rise, stand up for yourself and file an appeal. There will probably be a tight deadline to file the paperwork, and the dates should be included in the paperwork you receive. If you don't file on time, you will lose any right to challenge the increase.

253. I own a duplex and there is only one water meter. How do I charge the tenants?

You may not be able to. Depending on where you live, if the utilities aren't separated, you will have to pay the entire bill. It's easy to make this mistake, especially when you are a newbie. I made a deal once and didn't realize the meters weren't separated. I hadn't factored that into my offer, and I wound up having to sell the property because paying the utilities made the deal too skinny. Make sure you verify that each property has a separate meter before you purchase a property, or add the cost of the utilities into your offer. The good news is that you can fix this issue. When one of the leases is about to expire, hire a repairman to install separate meters, and then allow the new tenant to pay for her own utilities. When the second lease expires, you will be off the hook for the utilities. However, there are some municipalities that will split the bill for you. Call your water company to see if this service is provided and take advantage of it as soon as you can.

254. I have a very disgruntled tenant. Can I evict him because I don't like him?

This is every landlord's dream. Maybe we should start installing ejector seats into our properties. When a tenant pisses us off, we could push a button and they would be thrown out of the house. It would be just like a James Bond movie. Unfortunately, you can't get rid of tenant just because he is a jerk or makes you mad. He has to breach the lease, and then you have to go to court and get an order that allows you to force him out of the property. If you do your due diligence, you can weed out many of these people. Disgruntled people tend to be disgruntled everywhere, and they generally leave a lot of unhappy people in their wake. Spend some time with prospects before you allow them to sign a lease, and contact their references and employers. You can't eliminate all the bad apples, but you will weed out a bunch of them. And if you know someone who can build that ejector seat, send me his number.

255. What is second mortgage?

A second mortgage is an additional encumbrance on the property that is inferior to or secondary to the primary mortgage. If you are the borrower, it means you have two payments to make each month. If you are the lender, it's important to know which mortgage you have. If the buyer defaults and the property has to be sold, the funds will be applied to the first mortgage, and the second will only get paid after the first mortgage is paid in full.

256. I need cash now. Can I sell my lease-purchase to an investor?

Yes. Once you have a property under a lease-purchase agreement, it is treated like any other asset and you can sell it when you need to. If you get an offer on a lease-purchase and the numbers work for you, make the deal happen and put the cash into another property.

257. What is a flood zone?

Flood zone is a term that insurance companies use to determine how likely property in your area will be flooded in any given year. It's important to understand this because most insurance policies won't cover flood damage, and if you live in a high-risk flood zone, you need to have flood insurance. By knowing if your property is in a high-risk area or not, you can decide whether you need to buy flood insurance.

258. Do I need a survey when I purchase a property?

Generally not. This is one of those expenses I can't justify because of the prices I pay for my properties. However, if there were any questions about the property boundaries (such as if a neighbor's fence was leaning up against the exterior wall of the house I wanted to buy), I would request for a survey to be done. I would make sure the seller pays for it or deduct the amount from my offer. It's much cheaper to pay for a survey before you buy a property than it is to pay for you attorney to take the case to court after you own the property.

259. Can a tenant sign a lease before I purchase the property?

No. You don't have the right to lease anything before the property closes. Don't sign any leases until the closing has been completed. Most closings go off without a hitch, but it's not unheard of for a deal to fall apart at the title company. If you have a singed lease but don't own the property, you may end up paying for the tenant's storage costs while she finds a new place to live. Keep it slow, wait until you own the property, and have it rent-ready before you start showing it to prospects. You'll never regret taking it slow, but if you rush into things it can cost you a lot of money.

260. The seller changed his mind and wants to keep the property. Can he back out of a purchase contract?

If the seller is serious about backing out and not just negotiating, this is another area where you need to consult an attorney. If the contract is valid and the buyer hasn't breached the contract, the seller can't just change his mind. That's why we have contracts. But the bigger issue is, "What do you do?" In the worst case, you could sue him for specific performance, which means that the judge would order him to sell the property at the agreed price. But do you really want to be involved in a lawsuit that will take months to resolve? A better approach might be to negotiate a price for the seller to buy his way out. He would need to cover all of your expenses (and any real estate commission to his agent) and provide a reasonable amount of profit for your time and aggravation. Don't just walk away without getting paid.

261. What is quitclaim deed?

A quitclaim deed is a legal instrument that transfers any and all interest a person has in a property to another. However, unlike a warranty deed, a quitclaim deed does not make any representation that the person actually has any title or interest in the property. If there is ever a dispute about the title and you have a warranty deed, the seller has a duty to pay for any court proceedings to clear the title. With a quitclaim deed, you are on your own.

262. What does, "First one to the courthouse wins" mean?

Every property title has to be filed and recorded to be valid. Sometimes, there will be multiple deeds regarding the same owner and piece of land, and different people may make claim to it. In those cases, whoever files and records his deed first will have priority over the other claims, and he will be regarded as the owner. It may be possible for the other people who claim to have valid ownership in the property to get an order granting them possession and determining that their title is valid, but they will have to bear the expense and burden of proving that. This is why it is important to have a professional research the title of every property you buy. And if you ever have someone execute a deed to you, get it filed as quickly as possible. You want to be in the driver's seat if there is any dispute as to the title.

263. Can I put my investment property in a trust?

There are two issues to think about here. One is the proper business structure for your company, and the other is thorough estate planning. When you establish your company, your attorney and accountant will advise you on the best business structure for you. It will probably be an LLC or a corporation. They will be able to tell you which one will give you the most tax advantages and the most legal protection. Every time you buy an investment property, it should be owned by your company. Do not own the property in your individual name or you will defeat the purpose of creating your corporation or LLC. Trusts are generally used as an estate planning tool. The idea is that any property you own (such as your house or cars, or even your business), can be transferred to the trust so that when you die there will be no need to have those items probated. So to answer your question, your LLC or corporation should own all of your investment property, and then you should use a trust or whatever estate planning tools your attorney advises to protect your family in the event something happens to you.

264. I just went through a bankruptcy. When can I start buying investment property?

Start buying property today. But don't jump in the deep end too quickly. Make sure you learned from whatever caused you to file bankruptcy. Borrowing from a traditional lender may be a challenge, but don't let that discourage you. You will need to find some owner-carries or use creative financing, but you can get it done. Keep hustling and call on every FSBO you can find. Something will come along and you can start building your empire.

265. What is trustee's deed?

A trustee's deed is a deed issued by someone who has been appointed to act a trustee over a property, usually a bankruptcy trustee. When a person files bankruptcy, all of their property becomes property of the bankruptcy estate and is controlled by the trustee. If the trustee decides it is in the best interests of the creditors to sell any real property in the estate, he will use a trustee's deed to transfer the property.

266. What is a mechanic's or materialmen's lien?

When a contractor repairs your property, such as replacing the roof, it's important to make sure he and his suppliers get paid. If not, they can go down to the courthouse and file a materialmen's lien on your property. If that happens, you will have a cloud on your title and it will make it more difficult to sell it or to use it as collateral for another loan. Don't pay your contractors until you get a Lien Waver, which will protect you in the future.

If a contractor attempts to file a lien, you can use the Lien Waiver as a defense. You can find this form on my website.

267. What is a short sale?

A short sale is an incredible opportunity for investors. Short sales happen when a house is not worth the value of any mortgage or liens placed on it and the borrower doesn't have enough money to pay the difference. The borrower agrees to sell the property at a loss, which means that if you play your cards right, and find the right short sale; you can buy property at a substantial discount. But short sales can be a lot of work. They can take months to complete and often involve a lot of work. Make sure you factor the expense and time into your offers.

268. What does a loan broker do?

A loan broker is a middleman who helps bring borrowers and lenders together. Loan brokers charge a fee, and they help fill out the paperwork to make sure the loan gets processed. If you're having a hard time finding financing to buy new properties, loan brokers can be a great resource. I use a loan broker and love the guy. He handles all the details, and I can focus on finding new deals.

269. Can a bank sell my mortgage?

Yes. It's not uncommon for mortgages to be sold, and some of them are sold more than once. It can be stressful when you get a letter in the mail that says a different company owns your mortgage. Don't take this personally or as a reflection of your creditworthiness. To a bank, your mortgage is just another asset. If they crunch the numbers and it's more profitable to sell the mortgage than it is to service it, your mortgage will be sold. They won't think twice about it, and neither should you. Just keeping making the payments on time.

270. What is a due-on-sale or acceleration clause?

These clauses apply to people who sell property subject to an existing mortgage. When a seller transfers title to the new buyer, an acceleration clause gives the mortgage holder the right to make the seller pay the mortgage in full. They are relatively new, and are one of the side effects of the S&L craze of the 1980s. Almost every mortgage issued these days has an acceleration clause.

271. Can I buy a property that has several different liens like a tax lien and judgment lien?

Yes, but make sure you include the cost of the liens or judgments into your offer. You will have to pay them before you will have clear title, and you need to be sure these amounts won't make your deal too skinny. If you are savvy, you can make money on properties like this, but don't waste your time if the numbers don't work.

272. When I purchase a property can I put the title in my kid's name?

Sure, and you can also put it in your neighbor's name, put it in the name of your postal carrier, or use a random name you pull out of the phone book. The question is, "Why would you want to do that?" Your company should own every property you buy. Period. It's the only way to make sure you are protected and are able to take the deductions you are entitled to.

It's really not that difficult. Use your company to buy the properties and be done with it.

273. Can I research tile myself or do I have to use a title company or attorney?

You will need to have a title examiner research your title. It's the only way you can get title insurance or to secure conventional financing. I'm all for learning to do things for yourself, but title research is not one of those areas. There are too many traps and dangers, and you need to pay for someone to do this for you.

274. What is LTV?

LTV stand for "loan-to-value" ratio. Lenders look at this to determine the risk of a loan. It is calculated by dividing the amount of the loan by the value of the property. For example, if you need to borrow $55,000 on a $60,000, house the LTV is 92 percent ($55,000 divided by $60,000). Most investor banks won't loan money if the LTV is over 70 or 75 percent, so you have to know the LTV of a deal and how much your bank will lend before you apply for a loan.

275. Do I have to rent to smokers?

Nope. Smokers are not a protected class under the law and you can reject someone's application if he is a smoker. Many investors won't rent to smokers and have a no-smoking addendum in their leases. You will rent each of your properties to more than one tenant. People move because they get married, start families, are transferred by their employers, and because they want a change of scenery. So you always have to be thinking about your next renter. Smoke doesn't just linger for a few days and then go away. It seeps into the carpets and walls, and you can smell it for months or even years, after a smoker has moved out. And you have to repaint the walls more frequently because the nicotine stains everything. Plus, you'll wind up with burned countertops and floors. It just isn't worth it to rent to smokers. And if you own multiunit properties, you have an entire new set of problems. Many people don't want to live next door to smokers, and if you allow smokers you have eliminated a lot of qualified tenants who won't live in your complex. Snuff out these problems by not renting to smokers.

276. I just received a call from my tenant's bankruptcy attorney, and he told me the tenant can't pay rent. What do I do?

Bummer. This is pain in the butt. This can be a technical area of the law, and you shouldn't do anything without talking to your attorney. But here are the general rules. If you haven't gotten a judgment against your tenant, you can't do anything without the permission of the bankruptcy court. Once a person files bankruptcy, they receive an "automatic stay," which means none of the creditors can try to enforce any contracts or collect any debts. If you have already sued to evict the tenant and have been awarded possession of the property, the automatic stay doesn't apply, and you can proceed with the eviction. If not, you'll have to petition the court to lift the stay so that you can evict the tenant (assuming he has breached the lease). But this gets even trickier. During the course of the bankruptcy, the trustee appointed to the case will review all of the tenant's obligations to see if he can pay them. So even if you want to keep the tenant and you can't evict him, the trustee may decide the terms of your lease are oppressive and allow the tenant to move. Hopefully, your tenants will never have to file for bankruptcy, but if they do, stay calm and get as much legal information as you can from your attorney.

277. What is a triple net lease?

These are really sweet deals for investors, but you will usually only see them in commercial deals. I couldn't believe they actually existed when I first heard about them, and now I wish every lease was a triple net lease. Under a triple net lease, the tenant pays not only rent, but also insurance, property taxes, and maintenance costs. The tenant would still be liable for utilities and any other expenses related to the property. Essentially, the owner gets all the benefits of ownership with none of the burdens. Let me know if you hear about any of these. I'd love to get in on the party.

278. Is it possible to "over improve" my investment property?

Absolutely, and this is one of the most common mistakes newbies make. New investors tend to think they have to do everything they can to make property rent-ready. They buy the most expensive fixtures and they add every option they can. They rehab the property as if they were going to live in it themselves and not rent it to strangers. When you buy a property, you don't have to do everything possible. Your job is to make the housing clean, habitable, and to make sure you wind up with positive cash flow each and every month. Adding too many improvements is a sure way to blow your budget and keep your business from growing.

279. How can I save money on basic repairs?

The first thing to learn is that you will not save money by doing the repairs yourself. Your time should not be spent doing work you could farm out to a handyman for $10 or $15 dollars an hour. Your time needs to be spent putting deals together. The next time you feel tempted to save a few dollars by painting a living room yourself, think about this: Does the president of

Ford try to save a few dollars by going down to the garage and changing oil and filters on customers' cars? Or does he hire people to do that so he can focus on the big picture issues? Don't hold yourself back by thinking you have to do everything. Delegate the small jobs and you'll make more money. I try to have a list of three handymen for each type of job (plumbing, painters, carpenters, and so forth). You can find them by running ads on places like Craigslist or by asking other investors. The first one is the cheapest, and he can handle the basic stuff. He's the first guy I call when I need to get something done. If he can't do what I need, I move on to the second guy. He's a little more expensive and has more skill and experience. And if he still can't take care of things, I call the third one. He's the big daddy. If he can't do it, it can't be done. But he's also the most expensive, and I don't want to call him unless I have to. This helps keep my repair costs in check.

280. Am I required to provide smoke or carbon monoxide detectors?

Most states require landlords to install smoke detectors. If you don't have them, you could be fined by the authorities, and face civil or criminal action if something were to happen to a tenant if the detector could have saved them. But most places don't yet require carbon monoxide detectors. However, they don't cost very much and they are simple to install. Having safety features like these could be a great way to attract new tenants. Your tenants can even get smoke detectors for free from fire stations in certain areas.

281. I'm getting a loan and the loan officer keeps talking about points. What does that mean? Is there a difference between basis points?

"Points" is fancy way of explaining the interest rate you would pay on a loan. One point is equal to one percent. So if your loan officer is talking about five points, she means five percent. A "basis point" is 1/100 of a percentage point. It looks like a small amount, but when you are talking about a $40,000 or $50,000 loan, every point (and basis point) can mean hundreds or thousands of dollars.

282. Can I reduce the points being charged?

Yes. Like most things in real estate, if you are savvy and have leverage you can negotiate the points you are charged. Every point (or percentage of a point) is money out of your pocket, so pay attention to how many points you are being charged and reduce them when you can. Points are usually a reflection of your creditworthiness. You will pay fewer points when you have better credit and more when the bank is worried about getting its money back. One of the best ways to get better interest rates is to check your credit report and take care of any problems. If you have rough credit from the past, there's nothing you can do about that, but you can make a commitment to start paying bills on time. And you can also pay off any outstanding bills. The goal is for your lender to be able to pull your credit report and have confidence that you will pay back the loan. To get the best rate on your points, you should also have all of your financial information in order. Be able to document your income and expenses. If you show up to your banker's office with a shoebox full of receipts and an income statement written on a napkin, you probably won't get the best deal. But once you get a loan you can posture yourself to do better on the next one.

Make your payments on time, return phone calls from your banker, and be professional. When you have a working relationship with the bank, the people who sign off on your loans will have confidence in you and you can negotiate the points when you need to refinance or buy a property.

283. I was trying to close a multi-unit deal at the bank and the loan officer asked for a loan packet. What is that?

A loan packet (or loan package) is a collection all the documents that you will need to have your loan processed. These may include a credit report, a loan application, an appraisal, and documentation of your income and expenses.

284. I submitted two deals on two different properties and they were both accepted. What should I do?

Buy them both. If you've done your due diligence, both deals will make money and fit within your investment strategy. Your goal is to build an empire and to own enough properties to live a lifestyle most people only dream of. To do that, you have to create opportunities and then take advantage of them when they appear. Sometimes, you will have to say yes even when you aren't ready, and then make the deal happen. If you want to just sit on the sidelines and watch other people pass you in the fast lane, that's your choice. But when you want to be the one setting the pace, you need the courage to take calculated risks. Push yourself and you will expand your possibilities. But if there's no way to buy them both, sign off on the one that brings you the most cash flow.

285. Cleaning toilets is not for me, but I know investing in real estate could be a great opportunity. What can I do?

I don't clean toilets either. I also don't do windows, pick up dog crap, or carry out other people's trash. But the good news is you don't have to do any of those things to make money in real estate. In fact, you should hire people to do them for you as quickly as you can. Entering into a partnership agreement is a great way to reap the benefits of investing without being responsible for any of the work that many of us dread. Your partnership agreement should outline who is responsible for cleaning and maintaining the property and how the profits are split. Another great way to make money in real estate without doing any of the heavy lifting is to hire a management company. Management companies will lease out your properties, handle all of the maintenance, and take care of any necessary repairs. If you hire the right company, you just sit back and wait for a check to roll in each month. Of course, they charge for their services, but the freedom they offer can be worth the price.

286. Do I need to have an exit strategy when I start investing?

Yes. I am a glass half-full kind of person. When I put a deal together, I do everything I can to make it work, and I want it to succeed. But I have an exit strategy for every deal I do and every property I own. One of the greatest things about real estate is the flexibility. There are so many was to exit a deal over time, such as selling it for cash if I need money, refinancing it to cash out my equity, selling it on terms, renting it out, and holding on to it until it matures and selling it for a profit. Plus, not every deal is going to work out. There may be factors out of your control (such as a hurricane or tornado) that force you to get rid of properties, and you may make mistakes that cause other deals to fall apart. You have to be practical if you are a real estate investor. Don't get married to any single property. If it is better for your portfolio to get rid of a property, then do it and don't look back. Pull the trigger, learn what you did wrong, and move on to the next deal.

287. How do I calculate the square footage value of a property?

This can be one of the best ways to determine if a property is a good value, and it's simple to do. Just divide the price of the property by the square footage. For example, a $100,000 dollar home with 2,000 square feet is selling for $50 a square foot. If you compare the square footage values of several properties in the area, you will get a sense of what is a good value and what is overpriced.

288. What is GIM?

GIM, or gross income multiplier, is another great way to see if a property is a good value or not. It is determined by dividing the sales price by the annual rental income. For example, if you bought a house for $45,000, and you charge $600 per month, you would divide $45,000 by $7,200, which is 6.25. You want this number to be as low as possible because it represents the number of years it will take to pay off the property. GIM doesn't take into account other factors such as taxes, insurance, or utilities, but it's a great way to begin analyzing properties. If the GIM doesn't seem low enough, you don't need to crunch any other numbers.

289. What is the capitalization of net income?

This is a simple equation and is a great way to compare properties. You divide the annual net operating income (after costs) by the purchase price. If you bought a property for $60,000 and it clears $700 per month, you would divide $8,400 by $60,000, which yields 14 percent. The higher the percentage, the better the deal.

290. What are tax stamps and do I need them?

These are not what you use to send your payment into the IRS each year. A tax stamp is a stamp placed on certain legal documents before they can be filed, such as deeds. In some places, the buyer must pay the tax and affix the stamp to the deed before it is recorded. Subsequent purchasers can then look at the stamps to determine how much the current owner paid for the property. However, many places no longer require tax stamps, and some buyers intentionally pay a higher tax to make it look like they paid a higher amount for the property, so this is not the most accurate way to discover the actual sales cost of a property.

291. Do I have to provide appliances for my rental property?

No. We only provide stoves, and our tenants have to rent or buy refrigerators. I'm not that excited about running an appliance rental store, so the tenants usually find them elsewhere, although we do rent a few.

292. When I collect an application fee, do I have refund it if I don't rent to the applicant?

No. Your application should clearly state the fee is non-refundable. You will be amazed at how much work goes into processing applications, and you will earn every penny of the fee. Of course, the fee should be reasonable ($20 to $40), and the tenant needs to be given notice of the fee before he signs the application. Don't feel bad about charging this fee. If you don't value your time, no one else will either.

293. How do real estate agents get paid?

The big money for real estate agents is the commission they make when they sell a property. A good, motivated agent who wants to build his business will hustle to bring you the properties you want to buy, and this will make you both rich. However, some agents have started charging other fees, such as transaction fees, and this really pisses me off.

294. Do I really need to give my new tenant a lead-based paint disclosure pamphlet?

Only if you the house he is renting was built or rehabbed prior to 1978. This is another pet peeve of mine. I think that in order for a person to be impacted by lead paint, he would have to eat more of it than is in most houses. But the law is the law, and you will have to give a disclosure pamphlet when you rent an older home.

295. I went to my local REIA meeting last week. I had a bunch of questions I wanted to ask, but I was afraid of looking stupid. What should I do?

We have all been there. Trying something new is always difficult, and when you go to a meeting where everybody else seems to be an expert it's easy to think you will never understand or be good at it. But the only way to learn is to admit (to yourself and to everyone else in the room) that you need help. Don't let your pride or the fear of looking like a newbie get in the way of building your empire. At some point in time, we were all newbies, and there are at least one or two people in your REIA who had the same questions that you have. You will probably have the answers to your questions as soon as you ask them. Write down your questions before the next meeting, and think about your family when you stand up before the group.

When you remember why you decided to become an investor it will make it much less painful. And be sure to pay it forward when someone asks a question you can answer.

296. Should I ever let a tenant break his lease?

It may sound strange, but there will be times when you will pray for a tenant to leave. You will regret the day you met him and when you hear his name you will want to drive your car off a cliff. Regardless of how much rent he pays you each month it is never enough. If you ever find yourself in a position where you know it's time for a tenant to move onto greener pastures, don't hesitate to end the relationship by having him sign an early termination agreement. Of course, charge a reasonable fee to let your tenant out of the deal, just like your cell phone company would charge you to get out of your contract.

297. How do I make a "seller financing" offer?

A seller financing offer is one where you offer to buy a specific piece of property if the seller agrees to finance it. Whenever you make a seller financing offer, you should include all the important terms, such as the sales price, what the down payment will be, the interest rate, and how many months you have to repay the loan. Keep in mind that most sellers prefer for you to get financing on your own, and you will have to make a lot of offers before someone accepts one. Sellers who are interested in financing properties are most likely those who are about to retire, or who are leaving the business and want the security of a monthly payment without the headache of maintenance or dealing with tenants.

298. I've heard about homestead exemptions. What are they?

A homestead exemption is a legal right given to homeowners. It means that your residence is protected from being sold if you lose a lawsuit and have a judgment against you. The idea is to keep people in their homes as long as they can. It only applies to your residence and not your investment property, and it doesn't apply to tax liens or to materialmen's liens. But it's something you should know about in case you go through hard times.

299. Should I use a line of credit to buy investment property?

Seasoned investors use a line of credit (also known as a home equity line of credit or "HELOC") to make cash offers, close quickly, and save a boat load on closing costs. You pay for the properties with your HELOC, and thirty to sixty days later you refinance the deal by mortgaging the properties, pulling out some of your equity, and paying back the line of credit. The quickest way to build your empire is to leverage your money, and responsibly using a line of credit can be a great way to do this.

300. How do I get the bank to loan me the most money?

You have to remember there is difference between loan value and appraised value. Banks will loan on the appraised value or contract price, so when you make an offer you need to know what the property will appraise for. Your offer will hopefully be below appraised value, and when you take to the bank you can finance it for more than you paid for. And that means you will leave the closing with a check in your pocket.

301. I moved out of my residence and I couldn't sell it, so I am turning it into a rental. How long do I have to sell it and keep the proceeds tax free? Can I convert it into an investment?

What happened to all the softballs you were lobbing at me? This is a challenging question, so let me tweet my attorney and CPA and make sure I don't steer you in the wrong direction. You should probably contact yours just to make sure I have this right.

Here is the gist. You actually have to rent the house for more than a year before you can convert it to an investment for tax purposes. If you advertise the property for rent but never get a tenant, or if you rent it for less than a year, the property is not eligible for conversion. You will also have to get a credible appraisal of the property to determine its fair market value. If you are able to convert the property, you have three years from the date of the conversion to sell the property and keep the gains tax free. My accountant just tweeted me back and told me there are a ton of things to think about before you do this (including market conditions and what you need to cash flow on the property), so make sure you call your accountant before you try converting your residence into rental property.

TWENTY BONUS TIPS

1. Pull permits before you do any work. I once rehabbed a duplex, and after I finished one side it was brought to my attention that the gas line hadn't been used since 1989. In Oklahoma, any time the gas hasn't been turned on for over a year, you have to pull a permit and do a pressure test. I had already done some of the work, but I had to redo it in order to pass the test. If I had pulled a permit before I started, I would have saved myself time and money. And those are two most important things in my business.

2. If your bills don't add up, always ask questions. A plumber told me a story about an investor who experienced a spike in the water bill at one of his properties. He called the plumber to diagnose the problem. It turned out there were several leaks under the home, and when the plumber gave him an invoice the investor took it down to the utilities company and got a reduction on the bill. It's always worth the effort to ask. The worst they can say is no.

3. When you acquire new properties, change the normal locking door knob to a non-keyed passage door knob doorknob and add a deadbolt. Your tenants will no longer be able to lock themselves out. And make sure to implement a fee for "lock outs." Even if you use passage knobs and deadbolts, tenants will still lose leys. We charge $25 to unlock a property. If tenants know up front about the charge they usually think twice before calling us.

4. Use "cash for keys" as a way to gain early access to your property. What do you do when you have a deadbeat tenant or a tenant who has been

evicted but refuses to leave? It will cost you time and money to file an eviction or to get the sheriff to come out and forcibly remove the tenant. One great incentive for the tenant to leave is cash. Offer to pay the tenant directly if he hands over the keys and gets his stuff out immediately. It's also a great technique to use if you buy a foreclosed property that has tenants in it. Make sure the agreement is in writing and that it states a date and time the tenant will leave the property. You have to pick a dollar amount that makes sense. If it's cheaper to let the tenant stay in the property until the sheriff comes, then let that process work. Usually, $100 to $300 is a great motivator for the tenant to leave, and will save you cash in the long run.

5. Use a Realtor as a leasing agent. This may sound like a no-brainer to some of you, but I didn't start using Realtors as leasing agents until recently. I was having a difficult time leasing a property in an undesirable area, and I shared that with a Realtor I knew. He mentioned he does a lot of online marketing and would help me market my property. In a few weeks he brought me a tenant who was ready to start paying me rent. The Realtor charged me half of the first month's rent, but it was worth every penny because he marketed the property, had showings, took applications and pre-approved the tenant for me. Basically, he did all the legwork for me. I still manage the properties, but I am quick to have Realtors do the labor intensive work for me.

6. Use a mold addendum. An unfortunate trend I have seen lately and read about online is that tenants are using mold (or even just the allegation of mold) as a way to receive rent reductions or as a tool to intimidate landlords. Some unscrupulous people (not everyone is as honest and decent as you are) will threaten their landlords with a lawsuit over mold in the rental property. Be savvy and protect yourself from these

sleazebags. Have each tenant sign a mold addendum that states you have no prior knowledge about the property having any mold. You can find a free mold addendum on our website, thesavvylandlordbook. com. Of course, if you find mold on your property, make sure you have it removed as quickly as possible.

7. Always explain the eviction process to new tenants. If you read The Savvy Landlord, you know I really stress this point. When tenants are signing their first lease with you, go through the eviction process step-by-step. Paint a clear and vivid picture of what will happen if they don't pay their rent on time. Highlight the repercussions of being evicted and how it will follow them around for years. It will make it difficult for them to find a place to live or to get hired. Many tenants don't know the system and may be ignorant of the lasting consequences of eviction. They think they can just walk away from their obligations. I wish their parents raised them to understand integrity, but giving a refresher course keeps everyone on the same page and creates a high level of expectation that the rent will be paid on or before the first of the month. Period. There will be no exceptions, and each tenant should understand that when you hand him the keys to your property.

8. Submit a dual offer on your next investment property. A dual offer in real estate investing is when a perspective buyer makes two offers on the same property. One is a cash deal and the other one is on terms. Cash deals can be great for sellers. The take the money, sign over the deed, and the deal is done. But the right deal on terms can mean greater profit over time, and it also guarantees a steady income for the life of the deal. As a buyer, deals on terms help you leverage your money. You have more cash left in the bank after the deal is done, which you can use to buy more properties. If you submit both offers, you may wind up

with a seller-financed deal instead of forking over all your cash. You won't know unless you make a dual offer.

9. Make extra money by holding an estate sale. I knew an investor who rehabbed and flipped houses for a living. I ran into him one day at an estate sale. I thought it was odd when I saw him selling five different runner rugs. He told me when he finishes a rehab and puts it on the market; he holds an estate sale there to generate interest in the property and to sell all the stuff he has been buying at auctions and garage sales. Sometimes he makes more on the estate sale than from the profit he receives flipping the house.

10. Pit Lowe's and Home Depot against each to create a bidding war. I was rehabbing a property and I needed a pallet of tile. I went to Home Depot and got a great bid. I then went to Lowe's and ordered a pallet of wood flooring at the contractor desk (their prices have always been the best). I mentioned I was rehabbing a monster of a property and I had just gotten a bid from Home Depot for a pallet of tile. "We will beat our competitor's bid," the guy behind the counter said without batting an eye. "Yea, right," I thought. I entertained the guy and pulled out several bids I just received from Home Depot. True to his word, the clerk beat the Home Depot price and I saved 10 percent. I was already getting a 7 percent discount from Home Depot by going through the contractors' desk, so I wound up saving a grand total of 17 percent. The next time you have a big project save thousands of dollars by seeing if the store you use will match or beat a competitor's price. Do everything you can to see an ROI.

11. Investing in an IRA/Roth IRA can be a great tool to show your banker you are not always pushing the edge. I think there is always a bit of tension between bankers and investors. Bankers like to play it safe, and

real estate investors like to push the envelope with a tool called leverage. When I submit my financial documents to my banker, I always include information about my Roth IRA. I think this lets him know I understand a more traditional way of investing and that I have a micro-safety net. I think it looks good to my banker that not all of my investments are tied up in real estate.

12. Sometimes tenants are the real pests. Eventually, one of your tenants will complain about bugs. It costs $75 to have an exterminator come out and spray, so here is the procedure we have put in place to save us time and money, and to keep the bug problem under control. We gently remind the tenant about the notice in the lease regarding non-spraying for pests after taking possession. If they keep bringing the issue up, we tell them, "I have set up a $25 account for you at Home Depot. You can pick out the chemicals you would like to use and spray, bomb or lay traps in the property." This shifts the burden on the tenant. In fact, he may have even caused the problem. Usually what happens is that the tenant never makes it to Home Depot to use the account. He will either go to Wal-Mart and pay for the chemicals out of his own pocket or forget about the matter entirely.

13. When you install a window unit air conditioner, swap out the regular electrical outlet with a GFI (ground fault interrupter) outlet. GFI outlets have built-in breaker switches that flip if the current is imbalanced. They can prevent electrocution, fires, and damage to your electrical system. They are a small investment that can pay huge dividends.

14. Use a Yard Butler to help put signs in your yards. In Oklahoma, the summer heat bakes the ground and makes it nearly impossible to put your "For Rent" signs in front of our properties. We discovered a great tool to help with this. The Yard Butler Roto Digger is an attach-

ment for your cordless drill that digs a hole for sign legs. You drill the holes, and then drop the sign into the ground. You can also use this to plant flower bulbs, install sprinklers, and fertilize trees and shrubs. It's a great invention that will make your life as an investor much easier.

15. Use a staple remover to save your fingernails when adding keys to a key ring. As you build your empire, you will deal with more locks and keys than you ever dreamed of. Unless you have the claws of a giant lobster, putting keys on rings gets old after a while. Use a staple remover to open the end of the ring so you can slide a key on it. Your fingernails will thank you, especially when you own dozens of properties.

16. Use social media (such as Twitter, Facebook, and Pinterest) to do a background check on your next tenant. We live in a digital world. People love to post status updates and share pictures with their friends online. You can find a lot of information about many people if you know where to look. Search the name of your prospective tenant through the search bar of the most popular social media sites. If you see tons of pictures of her partying at her house you may think twice before allowing her to turn your investment into a nightclub.

17. Set the stage. Your office says a lot about you, and if you pay attention to detail you can reinforce the notion that you take the business of being a landlord seriously. I know a property manager who manages 234 single-family homes, and when he collects rent or signs a lease in his office, he usually places some unique item on his desk. These have included a police badge, a box of bullets, and even a pistol. I can't imagine what is going through his tenants' and prospective tenants' minds when they see those things, but I hope it's, "I swear to tell the truth, the whole truth, and nothing but the truth, so help me God."

18. Don't re-tile a floor or shower unless you have to. When tile starts looking dingy, consider hiring someone to deep clean the grout or to re-grout the tile. This can save you thousands of dollars. You can also improve an outdated room by adding a towel rack or replacing the light fixture and mirrors.

19. Look for answers online. Don't stress over managing your investments, real estate, tenants, or repairs. Real estate has been around a lot longer then we have been alive, and someone has had to deal with the same issues that you face. So when you have a question, look for your answers online. One of my garage disposals stopped working and I couldn't figure out why. I was bummed because I thought I had to either replace it or call a plumber to fix it, and I wasn't excited about spending the cash. I Googled it and found out that most or all garbage disposals have a reset button. I pushed the button and the disposal roared back to life. If you're not excited about using computers, go old school and call a friend.

20. Take care of yourself and don't get burned out. Here are a few thoughts to keep you going when you don't think you have the strength to go on. Real estate investing is long-term game. It's a marathon, not a sprint. Don't take it personally. It's a business and you will see a return when you are savvy and disciplined. Stay connected with other investors and call them to say hello. Get involved with your local investment club. Read. If you need a break, use a management company for a year. I did and even though she ran my properties in the ground I turned that into a positive experience. I was super motivated to bring them back and create a pristine cash-flowing machine. I wouldn't have the multi-million dollar empire I own now unless I had gone through that experience.

BONUS INTERVIEWS

Gary Armstrong

Please rate yourself as an investor, with 1 being a newbie and 10 being a full-time investor.

I am a 10, a full-time investor. I am also a CPA, but I am transitioning out of that.

How did you get into real estate?

Some of my friends from high school were buying properties and it intrigued me. I started casually investing about 1980. I jumped right in the fire. My first property was four city lots with one building which had eight shotgun houses. I made money off it for three or four years, but I didn't rent to the greatest people in the world. Those houses have all been bulldozed now, except for one building on the corner. When the local economy went south, I sold that. In fact, things were so bad I wound up declaring bankruptcy. I got rid of all my credit card debt, but kept a lot of the real estate, including an ice plant I owned near Northwest 16th and Classen Boulevard in Oklahoma City.

How long have you been a full-time investor?

About ten years, and I was a part-time investor for about a decade before that.

Did you manage the properties yourself?

Yes, but I wasn't good at it. I was terrible at screening tenants. I would rent to anyone if they had the cash in hand. That's not the way to go. I had some really bad tenants, and it left a bad taste in my mouth.

I finally started getting savvy. I tried to buy a sixteen-unit apartment complex for $50,000 from a bank, but they wouldn't finance it, and we didn't get the deal done. To me, that's typical. Banks don't always have the best vision.

About six months later I went back, and the apartment was in terrible shape. It had been vandalized and a bunch of the windows were broken. I went back to the bank and offered them $18,000 cash. I didn't have the money, and I was shocked when the bank accepted my offer. I loved the building in spite of the damage, and was excited to buy it. I couldn't believe I had saved $32,000 in a few months. I had to get the money and found an investor to help me, but that wasn't tough. If a deal is good enough, you can always find the money. That was a good learning experience for me. I had always bought owner-carries before that and always managed to overpay for properties.

That changed about 1990 when I bought a five-acre property with a house on it for $3,500 from the county at a tax sale. I thought about moving there, but I decided to sell it and put an ad in one of the local papers. I had hundreds of calls on it and sold it for $15,000 with $1,500 down. It was a fantastic return. I knew there were other properties I could buy for even less money and that I could make money selling them. Being an accountant, I understood the numbers and I enjoyed that part of the business. I bought a bunch of other properties where I paid $1,000 to $1,500 a piece, and then did lease-purchases for $10,000 to $15,000. It paid off for me in ten months. The only way I sell properties now is through owner-carries.

What are some mistakes you have made?

I really haven't had that many bad deals in Oklahoma. I bought some property in Detroit and that experience has been a disaster. I bought thirty properties up there, but only made a profit on one. I might break even, but I don't know. One of the deals turned out to be great and it's paid me back for the others. But even that deal is falling apart, and the new owners are behind on their taxes. It will cost more to keep the property than it is worth. I was a newbie in the Michigan real estate market, and I didn't realize the taxes were going to be so high. They are about ten times what they are in Oklahoma, and that blew me away. For an investor, that was a killer.

What advice would you give to someone starting out as an investor?

Be careful about over leveraging. It's easy to get in debt, but those payments come every month regardless of what happens to you. That's part of what forced me into bankruptcy.

Why did you choose to be an investor instead of an accountant?

As an account, you are limited by the number of hours you put in, and you have to show up every month to get your work done. As an investor, you can set your own hours. And your tenants are not your bosses, unlike the clients I had as a CPA. It was very liberating to start buying properties. It's been a great thing for me. And I am active and still buy properties.

What would you do differently if you had the chance?

I wish I hadn't learned to do any plumbing. I absolutely hate it. That way, I would have been forced to hire it out. You don't save any money doing it yourself, and it keeps you from growing your business. And avoid buying properties in small towns. They look at you like a foreigner and their inspectors will fine the crap out of you every chance they get.

What's your worst tenant story?

When I first got into the business, I used to go collect the rent, and I had to make sure to do it on the first day of the month. If I got there on the second, they would have spent the rent money on alcohol and couldn't have paid me. One of my tenants was paying his rent on time, but he eventually got behind and I had to evict him. When I finally got into the property, I realized he had rebuilt a car engine in the living room. The carpet was soaked with oil and fluids. But the worst part was that the property was infested with roaches and mice. They were everywhere, and when we walked in the mice scurried back to whatever holes they crawled out of. We bought a bunch of traps and set them out, and before we got out the door I heard them all go off. So we collected those and reset them. About thirty minutes later they were full again. At the end of the day, we had disposed of fifty mice. That was a miserable experience.

I know you do a lot of owner-carries. How are they working for you?

Owner-carries are great if you are on the selling end. I once had someone pay $15,000 down, make nearly $100,000 in monthly payments over the course of ten years, and then walk away. What's really nice is that I have resold that property for $220,000. I've had several owner carries that came back, but that is probably the best deal for me.

What are your long-term goals?

I'm still buying properties, and I want to get to a different point. I seem to have been stuck for a while, and I've had some opportunities to get in on some good deals lately. I've always done well at tax sales and I will keep doing that, but I'm looking for different ways to leverage my money. I won't leverage with debt, just the paper from owner-carries. I want to buy property for a dollar and sell it for five. That's the margin I want. I bought eight properties the other day, and it's a bit overwhelming. One of the problems of tax sales is getting clear title. But at a certain point in the future, the title will be cleared up. I have a great attorney who takes care of that for me.

What do you like and what do you dislike about being an investor?

I like leveraging money and the residual income. I sell a property and just wait for the check in the mailbox or, even better, a direct deposit. I get money without having to do anything. Most of the people who buy from me like me because I'm the guy who helped them buy a house. The return my investment is awesome. I hate plumbing more than anything.

Has there been a book that helped you?

Rich Dad, Poor Dad. I love that book. It was inspirational to me.

Commercial, multi-family, or single-family?

Single-family. Not everybody needs land or commercial property, but everybody needs a house. You have so many more customers if you sell houses, and you need customers to build your business.

Jason Windholz

Tell me about your background and how you got started in real estate.

I started investing in 1996, and went full-time in 1997. I was doing rehabs, and put a lot of time in them. In 2001, I moved from Dallas, Texas back to Tulsa, Oklahoma, and had to start over because I lost a lot of my contacts. Things were really slow. In 2002 I was elected to run the Tulsa REIA, because I had been involved in the Dallas REIA. At that time, the Tulsa club only had a few people who would meet in a restaurant, but it has grown since then.

My first property had eleven storage units and a little shop. I wasn't prepared to be a property manager, and started doing rehabs instead. In 2003, I bought a triplex to try property management again. I had a bunch of stuff going on in my personal life, and couldn't give it the attention it deserved. I wound up taking a five year break from investing after that.

In 2004, I started a moving company and put my real estate company on the side until 2009. But now the moving company is on autopilot, so I spend my time on real estate and the REIA.

I currently have six houses. I've only been buying one or two a year, so I cherry pick the best deals. When I started, I was buying fifteen or sixteen a year. Most of the ones I buy now are buy and holds, because there are so many deals out there that don't need to be rehabbed. I can find a lot of properties that are move-in ready and I don't need to fix them up.

I like to resell with owner financing, but the laws here are pretty tight, and if I can't sell it within thirty days, I go ahead and put a tenant in it. So I have more tenants now than ever.

How did you get involved in the Tulsa REIA?

When I moved back to Tulsa in 2001, I searched high and low to find an investors' club because the one in Dallas had been such a big help. I couldn't find one online, and I asked every real estate investor I could find about a club and was finally able to track one down.

There were only five or seven people who were regularly attending the meeting. I told them about what I had done in Dallas, and based on that I was elected president in 2002. After we got the Tulsa club up and running, the founders of the Oklahoma City REIA contacted me to help them get it off the ground. They knew about the Dallas REIA and how I helped the Tulsa club. Even when I took a break from investing from 2005 to 2009, I still ran the REIA. Joining a REIA is a great place to ask questions and meet people. Whatever challenge you are facing, someone has been through it before and can help you resolve it.

We now have a forty-five to fifty people attend the Tulsa REIA each month. When the economy was at its peak, we had about seventy, but it's fallen off. People were afraid to invest during the recession, but it's picked up.

What advice would you give to someone new to investing?

Be persistent. Pick one area and stick to that. If you are doing rehabs, renting, and wholesaling, it's easy to get spread too thin. Get good at doing one thing before you take on other types of projects.

What is your focus?

It has changed. When I did my first rehab, I got dragged through a three-month closing and the financing never came through. After that, I learned to finance the property with a hard money lender, do an owner-finance, and then sell the note.

In Texas, almost everything I did was owner financing. The laws there make it easy on investors and you can foreclose on someone almost as quickly as you can evict them. But in Oklahoma, it takes too long, especially if you are waiting on someone to come up with a down payment. In 2009, I decided that if I couldn't sell a property within thirty days, I would rent it. I had to rent my first property in Oklahoma for two years before I could sell it. We bought a property last year and put a tenant and they are still in it. I don't know if it's because I've matured, but property management seems to be working for me these days.

151

I want at least 10 to 15 percent as a down payment, but there aren't enough people to do that. And that's where the tenants come in. I don't want the property to be empty while I am financing it. I do wrap around mortgages or subject to mortgages, and I have to make that payment each month, so when I can't sell a property I need a tenant to cash flow.

What is your worst tenant story?

One lady filled out an application but she needed to get her money together. I had a really good feeling about her. Another family called and they came out and looked at the property. They didn't have the money either, but they had a motorcycle to trade, and it really caught my eye. I didn't have a good feeling about them, and when we went to the property, I noticed our signs were missing from the yard. I mentioned that to them, and they said they had never seen the sign. I was new and it never occurred to ask where they had found my phone number. It was a couple with two kids, and I got the feeling the parents weren't getting along.

When I showed them the garage, I saw my signs and wondered aloud how they got in there. One of the kids blurted out, "We put them there." They hadn't even signed the lease and were already lying to me. When they brought the application back in, the couple was separated but trying to get back together. The husband had lost his job but the wife still had her job. Even with all those red flags, I still didn't turn them away.

The first lady who looked at the house called me, but I really wanted the motorcycle. I told her I had someone else who had the money, but if they backed out I would call her. The couple gave me the cycle and moved in. They were the worst tenants ever and about six months into the deal I had to evict them. They filed bankruptcy, but it was a day too late to stop the eviction, although we did have to go through the bankruptcy court, which took another six months. We were still making the payments during this time. Most people will leave once we file with the judge, but these people didn't leave until they had to.

What's the best deal you've ever done?

I just closed on a house that I bought from a guy who inherited a house from his parents. Three years ago, it had been redone and had all new appliances and ceramic tile. The garage was converted into a living room, and has a building in back. It was probably worth $50,000. They had installed a bunch of extras, and I bought it for $12,700. It had a mortgage, but the balance was only $3,000. It was a decent neighborhood, but it was in a bad part of town. I lowballed him, and it took me by surprise when his counteroffer was only $1,000 over my offer. Before I could call him back, he called me and told me he was negotiable. He was really eager to sell, and I can't believe I got the property for such a low price. I now rent it for $650 a month, and it will be paid for in two and a half years. That was a great deal.

Why do you use hard money lenders?

I used conventional lenders when I started out, but there were too many hoops to jump through. My current lender only wants comps, but traditional lenders charged appraisal fees, and I had to pay for a survey, points, and lenders fees. On the short term loans, the interest I pay is pretty much the same as the fees I used to pay. If you keep the loan under twelve months or so, it's a better way to finance properties, but if you take hard money loans out for three or four years, the interest will kill the deal.

Are hard money lenders more common now than when you started investing?

Yes. It used to be easy to get a conventional loan with 3 to 5 percent down, but now you need 20 percent. Plus, your credit needs to be spotless. Hard money is easier. You don't have to have a huge down payment, and your credit doesn't have to be perfect.

Is there anything you would do differently if you had the chance?

Yes, I would have been stricter on my tenants. Sometimes, I had tenants who would pay the rent on time for about a year, and then they would start having problems. They would give me some sob story, and I would fall for it and let them slide. But they would never recover, and they became a hassle from then on. I've started being stricter, and I file eviction papers when people get behind. I don't cut nearly as much slack on rent as I used to.

What do you like about real estate, and what do you dislike?

I really like the freedom. I can set my own hours and take days off when I want to. You have to put in some long days if you have vacancies, but overall I don't work when I don't want to. I also like putting deals together with just my knowledge. You don't need money. I don't like when someone moves out, especially when it's a good tenant. I had one house where several people moved out, and I hated looking at that place because it made me think that I had to put the effort into finding a new tenant. But the bright side was that every time I signed a new lease, I made more money.

Are there any books you would recommend or that impacted you?

There have been a bunch of them. One of the best ones was called Texas Real Estate. It was a textbook and might have been written for lawyers and covered everything you might want to know. It taught me a lot. Most of the books I have read have covered the business side of things. I liked Rich Dad, Poor Dad, and Cashflow Quadrant. A good book I read recently was

How to Make Money in Real Estate in the New Economy by Matthew A. Martinez. It talked about a lot of the things that are going on recently, and it's a good, quick read. The Midas Touch was good, even though I don't like Donald Trump that much. I then read The Art of the Deal and Never Give Up and liked them. I've started to appreciate his knowledge.

What does your future hold? What are your goals?

I'm looking to be more active. I'm remarried and I have more kids, and they have motivated me. I don't have a set number of houses to own. I want to start buying five or six hoses a year, which will give me enough growth. I'm not worried about having a bunch of employees. I don't want to work too hard. That's why I'm an investor, to build freedom and wealth with knowledge.

Jason Windholz is the President of the Tulsa REIA, tulsareia.com, and can be reached at houseinvestor.com.

Pat Pointon

How did you get into real estate?

I was born into it. My dad was in the business since 1947. He primarily did planned subdivision development and built some houses, and I have always been involved in the business. I grew up in it. I did a few other things, but they were never far from real estate, such as owning a mortgage company, building homes, and building subdivisions. This business is really big, and you can learn to do a lot of different things.

I'm semi-retired now and not as active as I used to be. My son is taking some things over and I'm selling other things off.

How long were you a full-time investor?

About twenty years.

I understand you hosted a radio show called Real Estate Magic. Can you tell me about that?

I knew a guy in Fairfax, Virginia who was on the radio, and I saw how he could go raise private investment money. He could take that money and buy as many properties as possible without having to borrow from banks. I started the radio show to attract private investors. That allowed me to not be as dependant on banks as other people were. That was good because banks change policies depending on what is good for them. If you deal solely with banks, you can be back to square one in a heartbeat. With private investors, you make all the rules.

Plus, with private investors, there is no personal liability. The property stands for the entire indebtedness.

Have you made any investments lately you could share with us?

I own a 118 unit mini-storage business now, which is just like an apartment without the plumbing. The return isn't great, but the management is easy. I bought it from a bank that had foreclosed on it and used a private investor to fund it. We can expand it to 400 units over time. It's not a get rich quick business, but when you're older you can manage it fairly easily because there is not a lot to go wrong with it. It will also be easy for my heirs to manage, and as I gotten older I've started to think about those things.

At one time you had a mentorship program. Tell me about that.

I still mentor people, but I do it on a one-on-one basis. I used to do 10 or 20 people at a time. I did that for two reasons. First, people who heard my radio show were constantly asking to buy me a hamburger so I could tell them how to get into the business. It's too big of a subject to talk about over a burger. Second, I decided I wanted a motor home, but my wife objected. I had to find a way to pay for it to get her permission. The mentoring program allowed me to do that. Plus, I enjoyed mentoring and it was a good thing.

Most of the mentoring programs I have seen are rip-offs, but I always felt good about what I did. I took my students out to look at houses, and I told them if they wouldn't buy the houses, I would. One of my students made $20,000 on one of the homes. Where mentorship pays the student a real dividend is when it lasts a long time. I gave each student two days of classroom study, and after that you got a year of unlimited contact with my family and me. That was worth more than the weekend, because if you were out doing your first deal and you had a question, you could pick up the phone and call us. We would either answer your question on the spot or come out and look at the house. That was the real value.

What would you tell someone who was starting as an investor?

The first thing I would tell them would be to visit a REIA group. Get acquainted with the people who attend. A lot of those people go out and eat dinner after the meetings, and I would make some friendships and take advantage of that. A good mentorship program can be worth your time and money. Eventually, you have to get your feet wet. Some of the courses you see on TV make the business sound easier than it is. Look at those courses with a jaundiced eye. Ask people you know if they have tried them, don't just throw out a bunch of money. I went to one course where the first thing they did was teach the people who attended how to raise their credit card limits. Then, they convinced them to use the increased limits to spend

$10,000 or $20,000 to buy a course. That was stupid. You'd be too busy paying off the credit cards to buy any property.

I would look at the properties that are listed at the REIA meetings. There is usually a deal table where people offer properties for sale.

Tell me about your best deal.

I've had a lot of good deals. I bought an office building, and I wished I still owned it. A couple of insurance agents were in there together. One had retired, and the other was very wealthy and had been diagnosed with a terminal illness. He wanted to get rid of the building before his time came. His partner wanted to move to Florida. They had rented the property to a travel agent who had passed away. The property was in limbo, and neither one of them knew what to do. They put up a "For Sale" sign, I got the property for $114,000, and they carried the note after I put $2,500 down. I put in about $2,500 worth of sweat equity, and sold it a few years later for $175,000. That was a good deal.

I bought a thirty-acre piece of subdivision property once. I told the seller I needed to get a plat approved by the city before I could get a loan. I gave him $500 nonrefundable option money to buy it for $30,000. I went to a surveyor I knew, and after he gave me an estimate I told him I would double that, but he had to wait for the plat to be approved to be paid. In the mean time, I took the preliminary plat out to developers and sold options on the plots for $7,000 a piece. I took those to the bank, got the loan, paved the streets, and paid my surveyor. I never had any of my money in the deal because I had borrowed the $500 option money from my dad. I wanted to see if I could put the deal together without any of my money. That was another great deal. The return was pretty good. I probably cleared $140,000 in a short period of time. It was a perfect storm of market conditions, and it worked out well.

The storage unit I bought was a good deal. I bought it with no money down and left the closing with $7,000 in my pocket. Plus, I bought it for about half its value.

Do you have your real estate license?

No. I used to, but I don't anymore. I have no regard for the Real Estate Commission. They are very anti-investor. They think everyone should pay retail prices, buy every property in his own name, and when he sells it he should use a Realtor, and that cycle should continue. Without that, Realtors won't get paid and that's all they care about. The Commission says it exists to protect the public, but in my opinion that is manure. It's too restrictive to be a Realtor, and it doesn't help investors.

Do you have any goals?

Yes, I have several goals. I am completing some subdivisions I started. I want to expand my storage business to 300 units by the time I retire, and I want to be out of debt. I am a big believer in goals and I make written goals all the time. I have a "want list," which is everything I want, even if other people think it is stupid. About once a year I look at it and am amazed at how many things I no longer want or that I have been able to get.

Are there any books you would recommend or that influenced you?

I've read lots of books. I'm an avid reader and read about two books a week. The best real estate investment book I read was by Gary Keller, called The Millionaire Real Estate Investor. It was excellent, and I would encourage anyone to read it. I've watched a bunch of webinars also.

I have done them all, and if I buy anything from this point on it will probably be commercial. If I could buy anything right now, it would be a mobile home park. They are management intensive, but the return on the investment is staggering. I sold one I owned, and if I could find the right deal I would buy one today. They are that lucrative.

GLOSSARY OF QUESTIONS

60. My tenant claims to be a handyman. Should I let him do chores in exchange for rent? ....*pg 33*

61. My tenant just broke up with her boyfriend, and she told me she is moving out. She wants her deposit back. What should I do?....................*pg 34*

62. After living in my property for two weeks, my tenant informed me he is a registered sex offender and can't live within 100 yards of a school. He has to move. Should I give him his deposit back? ....*pg 34*

63. Do I have to have attorney represent me when filing an eviction? *pg 35*

64. We just had a major hail storm. Should I call the insurance adjuster and file claims for my roofs?... ....*pg 35*

65. My tenant's refrigerator stopped working and he expects me to pay for the spoiled food. Should I fork over the cash? ....*pg 35*

66. My tenant just bought a 60-inch LCD TV and asked if it's okay to mount a satellite dish on the roof. Should I let him? ....*pg 36*

67. My tenant's dog just jumped through the screen door. Should I charge the tenant for repairing it?...*pg 36*

68. The plumber just called me and said that the sewer line at one of my properties was clogged because feminine hygiene products blocked the line. Should I charge the tenant for the service call?............................*pg 36*

69. The plumber called and found a toy in the washing machine drain line. Should I charge the tenant for the service call?......................................*pg 37*

70. The tenant claims there is mold in the house and requests a mold test to be done. What should I do?...... ....*pg 37*

82. I evicted a tenant who left her washer and dryer behind. A few days later she called and asked for the clothes inside the dryer. What should I

192. I recently started investing in real estate with two partners. I put in 1/3 of the investment and should get 1/3 of the profit. How can I make sure they are honest with me regarding expenses for repairing the property

About the Authors

Steven R. VanCauwenbergh is a long-time investor in income-producing properties and has mastered the critical areas of purchasing, financing, renovating and managing real estate. He has authored several books and courses empowering people to reach their goals of financial freedom. He is a highly sought after personal coach and teaches his techniques in seminars across the country.

Walter B. Jenkins is the proud father of international hockey sensation Katie Jenkins. Before beginning his career as a writer and speaker, Walter was an attorney and sports agent. He now helps people turn their ideas into great books. In his spare time he enjoys studying tae kwon do, scuba diving, riding his bike, and training his German shepherd, Jake the wonder dog. Learn more at www.walterbjenkins.com.

Many Thanks!

There are so many people to thank since my last book. I hope I include all whose help I am grateful for. This book would not be a reality if it wasn't for my loving family and their encouragement; my dear wife Shannez' and my mother Linda for being by my side through the entire process. I would like to thank everyone who has contributed to this project, so here we go - Walter B. Jenkins for his grace and leadership, Elizabeth Hunt for art direction and interior layout, Jason Grotelueschen for input, Jason Windholz for editing and awesome suggestions, proof reading and love!, Carri Ferguson and Jeri Segard for proof reading, Dean Wendt for the voice, John Day to GO BIG! A special appreciation for Jeffery Taylor for giving me the opportunity to speak at the 12th Annual Mr. Landlord Conference.

I would like to thank all the interviewees for giving me
their time and wisdom.

Input, Support & Inspiration:

Devin Long - Trusted handyman
Steven Earp - Belief, drive, authentic
Greg Brister - Fulfilled a dream
Ken & Sharlene Monier - The reason I can
Zac McDorr - Voracious reader
Ben Shrewsbury - White collar ambition
Ed O'Toole - Loyal
Scott Smith - Holds my hand
Bryon Hanawalt - Entrepreneur
Donny Ho - Creative master
Dutch Revenboer - Realtor of Realtors
Kenny Malabag - My cousin
Linda Hamilton - Left hand
Pam Schrader - Closer

Bille Presnell - Diva
Delton Brown - I can do that
Alvin Smith - No one else
Carl Nelson - Details
Raymond Moya - Yes boss
Jacquith Farris - Gun on hip
Stephen King - Smiles
Brandon Bull - True whiz kid
Masie Bross - Empowering
Justin McGavock - Day one
Mom - I want to work at I-Hop
Shawn McVicker - Doing it!
Alex Albers - Stud

Recommended Reading

Life Changers -
Start: Punch Fear in the Face *by Jon Acuff*
Five Wealth Secrets *by Craig Hill*
Rich Dad, Poor Dad *by Robert Kiyosaki*
Millionaire Fast Lane *by MJ DeMarco*
Leading an Inspired Life *by Jim Rohn*
Think & Grow Rich *by Napoleon Hill*
Win Friends Influence People *by Dale Carnegie*
Slight Edge *by Jeff Olson*
Maximum Achievement *by Brian Tracy*
Creating Wealth *by Robert Allen*
E-Myth *by Michael Gerber*
Why "A" Students Work for "C" Students... *by Robert Kiyosaki*
It's Not About the Money *by Bob Proctor*

Build Your Library -
No Excuses!: The Power of Self-Discipline *by Brian Tracy*
Today We Are Rich *by Tim Sanders*
How to Win *by Mark Cuban*
The Enemies of Excellence *by Greg Salciccioli*
Dream Manager *by Mathew Kelley*
Drive *by Daniel Pink*
Compound Effect *by Darren Hardy*
The Answer *by John Assaraf*
Cashflow Quadrant *by Robert Kiyosaki*
Platform: Get Noticed in a Noisy World *by Michael Hyatt*
Seven Years to Seven Figures *by Michael Masterson*
The Seven Secrets of Slim People *by Vikki Hansen*
Failing Forward *by John Maxwell*
Erroneous Zones *by Wayne Dyer*
Winning Through Intimidation *by Robert Ringer*
Good to Great *by Jim Collins*
Tipping Point *by Malcolm Gladwell*
The Dip *by Seth Godin*
Awaken the Giant Within *by Anthony Robbins*
Parenting With Love And Logic *by Foster Cline*
Mentor: The Kid & The CEO *by Tom Pace*
Take Your Life Your Life Off Autopilot *by Tweet Coleman*

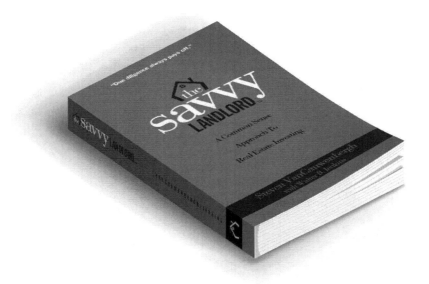

CONNECT AT:

thesavvylandlordbook.com

Freebies

Down-loadable Forms

New Products

Tips

Blog

Twitter: twitter.com/landlordbook
Facebook: facebook.com/thesavvylandlord
Email: info@thesavvylandlordbook.com

Knowing how to hire a contractor is crucial to your success as an investor!

Be empowered with the third book from The Savvy Landlord:

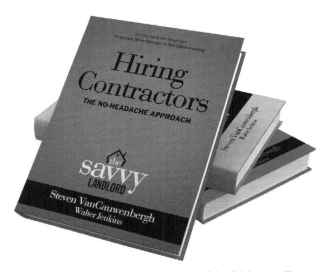

You will gain insight into the muddy world of blue collar servicemen. This book will guide you through the daunting tasks of finding the right contractor for your next project.

- **Negotiate like a pro**
- **Tips & Tricks**
- **50 Questions & Answers**
- **Pre-qualify contractors quickly**
- **Learn a new system in hiring labor**
- **True stories of getting the upper hand**

Get your copy today at:
www.thesavvylandlordbook.com

Resources

www.thesavvylandlordbook.com

www.mrlandlord.com

www.postlets.com

www.gosection8.com

www.buildium.com

www.shoeboxed.com

www.law.cornell.edu

www.legalzoom.com

www.google.com/drive

www.google.com/voice

www.hud.gov

www.biggerpockets.com

Don't have the time to read?
Listen!

Audiobook Now Available:

You will hear real life examples of real estate investment issues and how to deal with them.

301 AUDIO TRACKS, 3+ HOURS OF MATERIAL

MAXIMIZE YOUR LEARNING CURVE

Get your copy today at www.thesavvylandlordbook.com

Interested in learning more?

CALL NOW
405-633-1008

one-on-one coaching available

Made in the USA
San Bernardino, CA
21 October 2013